For my wonderful ♡ W9-CIQ-103 daughter

David and Renny

With all my love

Mother

Yesterday's Child

❦

Yesterday's Child

Helene Brown

M. EVANS AND COMPANY, INC.
New York, New York 10017

While this is a true story, several names
have been changed to protect the privacy
of living persons.

*M. Evans and Company titles are distributed in
the United States by the J. B. Lippincott Company,
East Washington Square, Philadelphia, Pa. 19105;
and in Canada by McClelland & Stewart Ltd.,
25 Hollinger Road, Toronto M4B 3G2, Ontario*

LIBRARY OF CONGRESS CATALOGING IN PUBLICATION DATA

Brown, Helene.
    Yesterday's child.

    1. Mother and child. 2. Brown, Helene. 3. Handi-
capped children—United States. I. Title.
HQ773.6.B76   649'.151'0924   76-00171
ISBN 0-87131-194-1

Design by Joel Schick

Manufactured in the United States of America

9 8 7 6 5 4 3 2 1

With love and gratitude
to my son David who
always understood

Chapter 1

𝓮

Y ou have to get me out of here on time, Jacques. I'm leaving for the Coast at four."

My hairdresser was waiting for me as I dashed into the Fifth Avenue salon between last-minute meetings with my associate editors and a conference with the editor-in-chief.

"Bonjour, Madame Brown. I will do my best."

I was wrapped in a blue smock and settled into a chair.

"And where are you off to now, Madame Brown?" In the few weeks since I had started having my hair done by Jacques, we'd talked a bit about my work and travels.

"I'm going to Beverly Hills and San Francisco. I'll be gone three weeks this time."

Jacques looked out at the bleak New York winter, the slushy streets, the dim gray sky. "How I envy you. Three weeks of sunshine. The sun does shine always in California, I understand. What a life you lead."

A life to be envied. Interior design editor of a national magazine. Travel. Photographing beautiful homes, meeting famous, interesting people. My work in print. Professional respect. A comfortable life, work that gives me everything I had always wanted, except . . .

"Madame Brown, did I mention last week that we have a new baby? Four months old now." In an excess of friendliness and fatherly pride, Jacques produced a handful of snapshots: his baby held by a beaming mother. The baby grinning up at the camera. I glanced through them and said admiring things. There was a box full of similar snapshots, yellowing a little now, tucked away in a closet of my apartment.

"He certainly is a beautiful child, Jacques. Enjoy him while you can. Kids grow up fast. It seems like only yesterday that mine were his age."

"Ah, you have children. I didn't know. How old are they?"

"My son is nineteen, my daughter is twenty."

The mirror in front of me caught the surprised expression on Jacques' face as he snipped delicately and expensively at my hair. "You do not look old enough to have grown children."

Every woman likes that kind of flattery; for me it confirms my hope that adversity had not altered me for the worse. "I married young, Jacques."

"Are they at home with you?"

It was a question that always brought a sudden clutch of anxiety to my chest.

That day I gave in to an impulse to alter reality just a little.

"David is at the state university," I said. "My daughter, Karen, is in London, studying fine arts."

"How fortunate you are," he said, "to have grown children and to be so young, with your whole life ahead of you."

There was some doubt in my mind about just what did lie ahead of me, but Jacques was satisfied. And for me, it was just what I wanted to believe. It was too late then to admit my white lie about Karen, to confess that I had denied the one undeniable reality of my life for the sake of impressing Jacques and the women sitting near me in the salon with the niceness of my life.

Later that day, on the DC-10 that was taking me to California, I strapped myself into a seat in the nearly empty first-class section and remembered with a twinge of guilt how easily I had spun my tale of my artistic daughter abroad and on her own. Then the guilt became a bit too much, and I knew I would be looking for a new hairdresser when I came back to New York. Jacques had had his answer, and I was coward enough not to want the question asked again. How different was the actual reality of my daughter that I had struggled with for twenty years: Karen Brown, cerebral palsied, mentally retarded, and deaf. How could I have answered Jacques or any casual acquaintance with a truth which I myself had been trying throughout her lifetime to accept? My lively, assuming, and imperfect daughter had grown to young womanhood, past the age I was when I gave birth to her, through years of suffering, learning, and growing, through years of turmoil for me, her brother, and her father.

I turned out the overhead light and in the cabin's darkness cried a few tears. Why couldn't it have been different, why not London and art school, why not everything I had wanted those many years ago? It didn't do much good to go over and over might-have-beens, but I went over them anyhow. What might Karen have been had she been born a normal child? What might I have been without Karen? Would I have had the wonderful life every young woman of my generation yearned for: marriage, lovely children, a house in the suburbs, a handsome and adoring husband? No hardships, no griefs, no doubts? Every movie I saw as a teenager, every story I read, every speculation about my future that issued from my mother's lips promised happy endings. All I had to do was be there.

I was there, right on schedule, but everything turned out differently than I had expected. There was nothing that prepared me for Karen.

Shortly after I separated from Karen's father, I had dinner with a man I had recently met, a divorced man who had a couple of children somewhere in the background. Desperate to keep a flagging conversation going, I asked about them.

"I have two boys," he told me. "Thirteen and fifteen. The younger lives with his mother. The older one was having some problems, so he's at a military school. We're really proud of the improvement in him."

I was so wrapped up in my concern with Karen that I let it pass without comment, but inside I was thinking bitterly that it would be nice to solve problems so easily. Send the difficult boy to a military school. As was my habit, I didn't mention my daughter, who at twelve was away at school where at last she was learning to become self-sufficient— walking, speaking in sign language, doing simple self-help tasks like dressing and feeding herself. I didn't even comment on my son, David, who at eleven was just beginning to overcome his own difficulties created by his handicapped sister. Karen was my precious, private burden, not to be shared with unfeeling strangers such as my dinner companion. We finished our evening, not regretting the sure knowledge that we wouldn't meet again.

It was Karen who was my whole life in those years. And

as it happened, only a few days after that dinner date, Karen's father and David and I were going to attend the parents' day exercises that marked the end of the school year at Karen's school. In spite of our separation, Karen's father and I attended school functions faithfully, hoping somehow to give her the sense that her little world was still whole.

This year Karen was to be the star of the school play, a fairy princess in royal robes and a crown, sitting in the middle of a circle of dancing classmates. We arrived early for the performance, joining the carloads of other parents and sisters and brothers. As I watched them drive up, I thought gratefully about how the school was able to create happiness and expectancy out of the misery and heartache that is too often the lot of families of the handicapped.

My Karen sat at the center of the stage, alive with excitement. She searched the faces of the audience until she found me.

"Am I going home with you?" she asked me in her personal sign language. "Am I going to sleep at home with you? Is my suitcase packed?"

"Yes," I signaled back. "Be quiet."

The faces of the audience around me were intent on the performance. Suddenly my eyes met those of a man seated a few seats away with a woman and a young boy. He gave a slight nod, a slight smile, embarrassed and understanding. The man I had had dinner with did not have a son at military school. His son was up there on the stage, a classmate of Karen's, physically or mentally handicapped in some way. Like me, his father had chosen the easy way out of a conversation about our children. I had not mentioned my daughter, while he had given a convenient lie about a child with behavioral problems being away at military school.

(5)

That was his solution, as it was mine—the fantasy we both wished was reality.

The reality of Karen, hopelessly damaged, yet who radiates a shimmer that lights up her whole being—gleaming teeth, shining hair, aquamarine eyes edged with thick dark lashes. Karen was at her loveliest in her teenage years, filled with exuberance and life. Only now in her twenties is she losing some of the freshness of youth as years of life in institutions and schools take their toll, leaving her touched with maturity of a sort, with sadness and resignation.

"Karen, what in the world are you doing?" I remember asking her on one of her recent visits home. She emerged from the bedroom wearing a pair of high-heeled shoes I had just bought for myself. "You can't walk in those shoes." She watched me carefully, understanding me through a combination of lipreading and sign language.

She looked down at her crippled feet in those impossible shoes, then laughed as she saw me laughing.

"P-p-p—" She tried to say *pretty*, a word an early speech therapist had taught her.

"Yes, they are pretty, but they are Mommy's shoes. You can't walk in them."

Ignoring me, Karen continued to totter across the room toward me.

"Karen, you cannot walk in them. You will fall."

Her laughter stopped. She looked at me pensively, trying not to understand what I was saying; but she knew. She knew that I could wear those shoes. She knew that she should be able to wear them too. She wanted to wear them. They were pretty. And she knew that she couldn't.

We looked at each other across the room, and I caught a glimpse of the frustration of her life. Somewhere beyond the limitations imposed by her physical and mental disabilities was the knowledge that she wasn't like other people, like her mother, and she wanted to be like them.

In Karen, wearing a pair of my shoes, I saw the frustration of my life, which will haunt me no matter what effort I make to outgrow it. The best I can do is learn to strike a balance between the irresistible pull of dreams and the harsh substance of life itself. I want Karen to be whole and perfect. I want my life to be serene and beautiful. But no matter how I strive to accomplish it, none of it is possible.

To serve two masters—the dream and the reality—means being torn apart. By a pair of shoes. By an idle question. By a beloved child who knows she wants more than her life has given her, as I wanted more when I was her age, as my mother and grandmother wanted more from their lives.

Chapter 2

❦

My GRANDMOTHER, Sara, used to sit in her little apartment in Brooklyn and tell me how, when she was a girl in Russia, the Czar would send a jewel-encrusted carriage to her farmhouse to bring her to the palace to sew for the Czarina.

"I was a beauty then, twelve years old, curls in my hair," she would tell me as she fashioned herself a satin blouse from a forty-cent remnant. "I dressed in my best clothes and the carriage would come, drawn by beautiful white horses. Then I would sew gowns for the Czarina, gold and silver cloth."

"And why did the Czar choose you, Grandma?" I would ask each time.

"I was the most beautiful girl in the village, and already I was known as a fine seamstress. The Czar's emissary was passing through the village and saw me. . . ."

It was a wonderful story and I never tired of it. I recently asked a cousin if Grandma had told her those stories when she was young.

"Of course," my cousin said. "But we never believed them."

I believed every word.

While my grandmother may not have had the life she fantasized to her grandchildren, she did have a remarkable talent for creating a better life for herself than she was entitled to in her circumstances.

It wasn't a very promising life to start out with. As was the custom in those long-ago days, she was promised in marriage by her father, who chose the man she was to spend her life with.

When she and her husband reached America just before the turn of the century, they settled in Brooklyn and filled their cramped apartment with eight children. That might have been all the story there was, except for that wonderful romantic streak in her that made her the Czarina's seamstress in her memory and in mine turned her into a close approximation of a Russian grand duchess.

I still see a tiny, commanding figure dressed in silk tucked blouses and elegant, sweeping gabardine skirts run up on her treadle sewing machine, her luxurious hair (Karen's hair) piled high on her head.

When she entered a room, leaning on her cane, she made her presence felt. She had a flair for beauty and life that was lacking in my grandfather, who sat at a sewing machine in a Seventh Avenue sweatshop all his life. It was lacking in her children, my numerous aunts and uncles, but she had passed it on to Esther, my mother.

Like Grandma, my mother was a woman of style and charm. It's a wonder to me that her taste for music, beauty, and fashion flourished in that crowded Brooklyn apartment.

In her youth, Mother was slim and barely five feet tall. She had luminous blue-green eyes, high cheekbones, a patrician nose and looked like anything but the daughter of poor immigrant parents. She wanted to be different from her brothers and sisters. She wanted to be better dressed, better spoken, living a better life than she could find in Brooklyn. All the children in the family had to leave school to work; Mother became a salesgirl.

"A *salesgirl*? I was never a salesgirl. I was a millinery buyer," she told me later. But she had been a salesgirl first; only, by her later years, she had become too proud to admit it.

The badly set broken leg that forced Grandma Sara to walk with a cane for most of her life came about, so the family legend says, when a horse and buggy she was riding in overturned. Many years later, the case (against the horse, perhaps; it was never clear) came to court, and my mother, then a young woman in her twenties, took Grandma to the courthouse every day for the trial. In the corridor outside the courtroom, Esther bumped into a young lawyer who took one look at her and was smitten. The romantic story of my mother's first meeting with my father was another family legend I never tired of hearing.

My father was then a promising, twenty-eight-year-old lawyer, the son of another poor immigrant who had settled in Philadelphia. Whatever the truth of my parents' first meeting (no more is heard of the court case), my mother fulfilled her modest dreams by becoming the wife of a lawyer and budding politician. They lived in Philadelphia where she had prestige, comparative affluence, and a grand social plan. In the late thirties, we must have been poorer than my memory of our life, yet my earliest recollection of my mother is one of her sitting at the full-sized grand piano that took up half of the living room, swathed in flowered chiffon and playing "At Dawning," one hand gracefully crossing the other in sweeping gestures.

Where did we get the servants we were never without? How could we have a car when no one else in our circle had one? My mother had furs and jewelry and beautiful clothes. We covered the elaborate mohair furniture with sheets each summer and went to Atlantic City. Mother saw to it that her only daughter had every advantage that she herself had been deprived of. She dressed me up and fussed over me and curled my hair and sent me to ballet lessons, piano lessons, flute lessons, acrobatic tap dancing and elocution lessons.

Was it all my imagination? My brother, three years younger than I, remembers much the same thing.

I know my father spoiled me outrageously. I was convinced that I was the prettiest, smartest, most talented little girl in the world. I was everything I ever wanted my own daughter to be—unique and beautiful, with the world waiting for me.

Until my father died at forty-four, on the brink of making his fortune, leaving us with only the unfulfilled promises of a prosperous life, I never had a day's adversity. Thanks to my mother's extravagances, we lived like royalty in a poor neighborhood that was my father's ward as city councilman. Overnight, as the story so often goes, our lives changed completely. The family, which had been headed by a busy lawyer and rising political figure, became a directionless huddle of three. My mother was incapable of dealing with a hopeless situation: no insurance, no savings, nothing.

Grandma Sara, leaning on her cane, led a delegation of uncles from New York to Philadelphia for a family council.

Mother knew how to direct the maids and buy new furniture. She lived well and dressed well. But she didn't know a thing about maintaining a big house and a car and two young children—without a penny.

"There must be something you can do," they told her. "Look at this big house. Turn the store in the front of the house into something."

Our house had a store where my father had a private office and waiting room for nighttime office hours with constituents and clients.

"You don't need this big house," they said. "You can start a business in the store and turn the rest of the house into apartments. They'll pay the mortgage and give you three something to live on."

We opened a dry-cleaning business which the family thought Mother could surely manage. Why a dry-cleaning business, I still wonder. There was a long-established cleaner and tailor on the same block. My mother had seen to it that we lived so differently from the rest of the neighborhood that we weren't an integral part. With my father gone, there was no special goodwill for us, and business barely trickled in.

In another overnight change, the office became a store, my chintz and ruffled bedroom disappeared to become part of the series of small apartments our house was turned into. The three of us crowded into a two-room apartment. While I finished high school, I worked in the shop every afternoon, writing up slips and tagging clothing, humiliated to be reduced to handling the dirty clothes brought in. My brother, too young to be much help, played in the streets with his friends. My mother was overcome by her grief at losing both her husband and her life of luxury.

The dry-cleaning business was not a success.

Mother's health started to decline—a series of constant,

undiagnosed illnesses and a steady gain in weight that soon became obesity. We moved out of our chopped-up house, away from the neighborhood where we were outcasts, and Mother took a job in a dress shop. She never knew how to adjust to our poverty; she just ignored it. New furniture appeared in our new apartment, and with it, the bill collectors. With Mother at work all day and suffering through the evenings in pain, the responsibility for her, for my brother, for the household chores, for fending off the collection agencies fell to me. I would come home from school with homework to be done, yearning to be like other teenagers—dates, dresses, parties, and nothing to worry about except boyfriends and exams. Instead, I was the head of a pathetic household, robbed of all youth, all joy, all hope.

I was torn apart by the events of these years. I was accustomed to a certain kind of life, and I had definite expectations about the future. When my father died, nothing prepared me for the turnabout in my life.

"Nothing worse can happen to me," I used to think in the night as I rode to a hospital in a taxi or ambulance with my mother crying out in agony beside me.

"This will all go away and everything will be all right again," I used to say over and over to myself as I sat through long nights in hospital waiting rooms.

It didn't go away, but things changed.

"Helene!" A familiar cry from the bed next to mine. "The pain. Take me to the hospital." My brother, sleeping in the living room of our small apartment, had learned not to hear those cries.

It was a snowy night, and the taxi was a long time coming. I helped my mother down the ice-covered steps to the waiting cab, struggling to support the overweight, suffering woman my slim, beautiful mother had become.

This is not what life is all about, I thought; my mother,

my brother, and me struggling to survive. I can't bear it much longer.

While my mother suffered through another hospital stay, the doctors unable to find a reason for her pain, my uncles reappeared from New York.

My Uncle Bill said: "You and your mother and brother are coming back to New York with us. You'll live with your grandmother until you get settled."

To me, escape from Philadelphia seemed like a miracle. Never mind about more school and the college boy I fancied myself in love with. New York was going to be a new start for me. The grass just had to be greener there.

Please let me find a husband; that will be the answer to everything. Prayer was not my strong point, but I was willing to try anything. So I prayed for a clean-cut, handsome, rich, loving man while we packed up to leave Philadelphia.

Uncle Bill, with whom I drove to New York, seemed to have the same idea. (Although he was probably less concerned about my emotional happiness than about getting at least one of Esther's burdens off his hands as soon as possible.)

"Too much school is no good for a girl, a waste of money," he said. "The smartest thing you can do is find a husband to take care of you."

I had to agree. Uncle Bill was full of good advice.

"And if you want to meet men, get a job in the garment district," he told me. "There are lots of young salesmen around. I see them every day."

Uncle Bill and all my mother's other brothers had prospered as sportswear manufacturers in New York, so of course they thought there were a lot of potential husbands for me running around Seventh Avenue. If they had been stockbrokers, they would have sent me instead to find a job (and a husband) on Wall Street. By the time we reached

New York, I was convinced that hordes of glorious men were lining Seventh Avenue, waiting for me.

Armed with a string of summer jobs and an extensive background in acrobatic, tap, and piano lessons, as well as a vision of myself as someone out of a Rosalind Russell career-girl movie, I presented myself at the first opportunity at an employment agency that catered to the garment district. I was so eager to get started on my romantic adventures that I scarcely glanced at the crowded little apartment in Brooklyn which my mother and I were to share with my aging grandparents (my brother had stayed behind in Philadelphia to finish high school). The two querulous old people and my ailing mother and the sofa that made into a bed for me didn't mean much. I wasn't going to be there long.

I was sent to a large textile firm for an interview. With my expectations of a rosy future, it was inevitable that when a young man walked briskly through the office where I was waiting for the personnel director, I felt my heart turn over. He was the man of my dreams, and I could have died of love on the spot.

The young man disappeared down a hallway, leaving me with damp palms and a throbbing heart. It had happened to my mother, hadn't it, in the hall of the courthouse? Well, it had just happened to me too. Never mind that he hadn't noticed me; he would, if I got the clerk-typist job I was being interviewed for. I must have overwhelmed the personnel people with my enthusiasm for their company, because in spite of my astonishing lack of business skills, I was hired.

I went home to plan my life with this unknown man, whom I had decided I was going to marry.

Chapter 3

❦

I HAVE a fondness now, some twenty years later, for the young woman who made plans for her future after the chance glimpse of a handsome stranger. She knew she was right. She was so sure of everything in those days. In that moment, in the weeks of silent love that followed, the misery of my life after my father's death evaporated. I was back on the path for which I had been intended all along.

After all, life was supposed to be pretty and nice. Little girls growing up in the forties and fifties were assured of an orderly progression of events stretching into the future: frilly dresses, dates, a boy you wanted to kiss more than any other, marriage. A couple of picture-book children, shiny, waxed floors, and love, romantic love, that survived everything, even adversity (whatever that was).

The young woman I was knew for a certainty that the only reality was the happy life. A flaw in the pattern was unthinkable. My father's death had been a mistake, the tragedy that strikes once and never again. Another such flaw seemed impossible, even when in the next few years it was apparent that my life was far from perfect. My tears, our suffering, the frustration and desperation that deepened until they colored every moment of my life—none of this was *real*. Beyond the horizon everything was all right. Badness and ugliness would go away.

I am fond of the young woman who rushed home from her job interview and told her mother: "I saw the handsomest man today, and I'm going to marry him." I like her because she lived then, for a few brief months, in a rosy world where dreams did come true. It is nice to be able to look back on my innocence.

"Who is he? What does he do?"

I didn't know. I didn't know his name or if he were already married. I didn't know what his job was, but someone that handsome must have a wonderful job.

For all her devotion to her lost life of luxury and her willingness twenty years before to heed the call of romance in a shabby courthouse, my mother was not impressed by my announcement.

"Who is this man? You weren't brought up to marry just any man." I had been brought up for a millionaire, at least. "Did you talk to him? What did he say?"

"No, I didn't talk to him." Cinderella doesn't have to talk to Prince Charming.

"Then what makes you think you're going to marry him? Who is he?"

"Just a man. I know I'll marry him." I sensed this wasn't

the time to tell her how little I knew about him. She'd come around soon enough.

I reported for work on Monday in a lovesick daze and spent the following weeks in a state of euphoria and anticipation of running into this man.

I repeated over and over to myself each night what I knew about him: He's older than I am, almost thirty. (I was nineteen.) He has such good taste. He's so attractive. His name is Richard.

I lived on those dreams of the future. It was springtime and warm and the birds were singing. I slept on the sofa bed of my grandparents' apartment and longed for this man who would take me away and make me happy forever.

"If I can only make him talk to me, I know we'll get married."

I joined the office bowling team on the chance that he'd be there. I had looked at my long fingernails and decided to sacrifice them for the sake of bowling and my future marriage.

There he was, the first night the bowling team got together. He spoke to me. In three minutes I managed to let him know that I had just moved to New York from Philadelphia, I knew no one, I lived in Brooklyn with my grandparents and widowed mother, I had just had my nineteenth birthday—and I was absolutely available.

"What do you do with yourself?" he asked.

The truth was, nothing. "I don't know New York at all," I said. "But I like to walk around." I used to leave the office after work and walk up Seventh Avenue to Central Park South. I'd sit on a park bench and look at the Manhattan skyline and dream about the wonderful life waiting for me. Then I got on the BMT subway for Brooklyn.

"I like to walk, too," he said. "We'll take a walk sometime, OK?"

I was ecstatic.

The very next night he was waiting for me in front of the office building. My romance was getting into high gear. He was so handsome that I was shaking.

We walked that night and the next and many after.

Meanwhile my mother fumed.

"What do you mean, you love him? Who is he? What does he do?"

"I don't know. He works at my company."

"How much money does he make? Who are his parents?"

"I don't know."

A girl who has been raised for something grand by a woman like my mother does not answer with "I don't know." You fell in love with someone you knew could provide for you.

I told my mother that none of that made any difference. I was in love with Richard. I had to be. If you wanted to kiss a boy, that meant you were in love. I wanted to kiss him, so I must be in love with him. But my mother was *not* in love with Richard Brown, nor the idea of him.

He asked me to go to Pennsylvania to meet his parents.

My mother was frantic. "Don't do anything serious, don't make any promises," she said. "Look everything over and see how he lives and what his parents are like. Don't make any commitment. You don't know what you're doing."

My future mother-in-law didn't seem especially interested in meeting the nineteen-year-old girl her twenty-nine-year-old son had brought home. She must have been as taken aback by the prospect of me as my mother was of Richard. But my love was too great to be dimmed by an unenthusiastic welcome. Then, as we got ready to return to New York, he asked me to marry him.

Suddenly I was engaged, and like the movie script I had

been living in my mind all those weeks, he whipped out a two-carat diamond ring and slipped it on my finger.

When my mother found out, she was distraught.

"I told you not to do anything."

How could I explain that you don't turn down the man your heart beats for, the only man you'll ever love. It didn't occur to me that he was the only man I had ever loved —so far. My mother (and his, no doubt) knew better.

"What is his family like?" Were they up to her standards?

"Oh, they're very nice." I thought somehow that my mother wouldn't think so.

"What is their home like? What does his father do?"

"It's a nice place. He's some sort of businessman." No, it wasn't at all like our house back in Philadelphia; his father was not my father.

"Let me look at your ring again."

The size of the diamond encouraged her. I was too happy to allow my mother's material concerns to spoil my romance.

Two months later, we were married, and three months after the wedding, I was pregnant with Karen.

Chapter 4

I AWAKENED SLOWLY, unable to comprehend at once where I was, unable to focus on my surroundings. I kept sinking back into a half-conscious state. But I sensed that something wonderful had happened.

Then I knew where I was and what had happened. I was in the hospital, and I had given birth a few hours before to a healthy, beautiful baby girl. I had a fuzzy recollection of holding her for a minute while my obstetrician bent over me.

"It's a girl, Helene," he said. "Just what you wanted."

Then I slept.

I had wanted a girl. The unexpected pregnancy had hardly startled me; I was just progressing with my dream life a little faster than I had planned.

Somewhere down the hall a baby cried and I heard the sound of brisk movement outside my room. I sat up in bed, fully awake. In a few minutes the nurse would bring my baby and I would hold her again and feed her for the first time. My roommate was already cradling her son, born within minutes of my daughter.

Then abruptly the corridor was silent. There were no more footsteps, no crying infants. They had forgotten to bring my baby from the nursery. They'd discover their mistake and bring her . . .

I dozed again.

Richard and I were poor, but we were happy, in the traditional way. We had no plan for our life; we didn't seem to need one. For me, it was what life was supposed to be: housekeeping, marketing, sending my husband off to work each morning, visiting parents and grandparents on weekends, getting acquainted with neighbors. All of a sudden, I was like other people. I had roots again. I had a husband I loved, a home of my own—half-empty apartment that it was—and then one day, I had a child coming.

It was right for me. I was meant to be a wife and mother. And perfection, that extra something, was (it had to be) just round the corner. When Richard made more money, I'd fill up the apartment with all the beautiful furniture and frills I longed for. Soon, when we had time, Richard and I would learn to laugh at things together, to comfort each other when we were sad, to enjoy life when we were glad.

And my child, already "Karen" to me (she was named for a grandmother whose name, Kate, seemed too old-fashioned), would put the final stamp of authenticity on my life.

The prospect of Karen erased the tiny stirrings of disillusionment that once in a while troubled me during the first months of marriage. What difference did it make if each day just happened to Richard, while I wanted each day to be different and interesting: new food on the table, something new in the apartment, new people to socialize with. He was so much older, he must be right. I adjusted myself to please him.

In spending hours talking about our coming baby, watching and waiting, painting a secondhand crib bright yellow, we found true intimacy for the first time. My mother forgave Richard the sin, in her eyes, of loving and marrying her daughter. She joined in our excitement about the baby, her first grandchild.

The hospital corridors were still silent. I rang for the nurse, but no one came. I rang again and again, panic coming over me. Finally I crawled out of bed and staggered to the nurses' station at the end of the corridor.

"Where is my baby?" I said in a voice I didn't recognize. "Where is my baby?"

"Your baby had to stay in the nursery, Mrs. Brown. She's a bit fussy today. We've called your doctor, and he's on his way in."

"I want to see her," I said, almost incoherent.

"You may see her if you like."

Two nurses walked with me to the nursery. Why two? I wondered. What does *fussy* mean? She was all right earlier —pink and tiny and quiet.

"Bring the Brown baby," one of the nurses told the nursery attendant while the other stood beside me.

An incubator was wheeled up to the window.

"There's some mistake." I could barely speak. "I'm Mrs. Brown. I want to see *my* baby. Please bring her."

The creature in the incubator was lying on her back

writing, her arms and legs flailing, her face red and contorted, her back suddenly arched in a convulsion. I stared unbelieving at the grotesque mockery of the infant I had held only a few hours earlier. Where was my beautiful, perfect daughter?

"Take it away," I sobbed, "take away that thing. Please, please just bring my baby."

"This is your baby, Mrs. Brown."

It was horrible and shattering, and I was all alone. Karen's birth in the early morning hours of Sunday, October 4, hardly gave Richard time to glance at his new baby daughter before he left for Pennsylvania for a week in court involving an accident five years before.

He held me for a moment, with tears of joy in his eyes. "We have our little girl, honey," he said. "Our Karen is here."

Then he was gone.

When next I awoke after seeing Karen for the second time, my mother and doctor were hovering over me. I saw the doctor's haggard face and my mother's red-rimmed eyes, and I knew that the nightmare I had been having was real.

"Dr. Drake, tell me what's the matter with Karen."

He held my hand. "Helene, dear, please try to stay calm. Karen has a slight irritation."

"Irritation? What kind of an irritation? Where?"

"In the brain." He spoke almost inaudibly. "We're doing everything we can to find out what's wrong. The Chief of Pediatrics will be seeing her. Try not to worry."

I looked at my mother; she looked very worried.

What had happened? I lay back stunned. I was a healthy twenty-year-old woman. I had had a normal pregnancy. My knowledge of medicine was limited, but a brain irritation had to be serious.

"We can't tell Richard," I whispered to my mother as I started to slip back into a drugged sleep. "Not over the phone, not until we know something definite."

Mother sat beside me and we both wept for my tiny child.

The next day a whitehaired, grandfatherly man appeared at my bedside. He was Dr. Cole, the Chief of Pediatrics.

"We have a team of doctors examining your daughter."

"Can you tell me anything?" My tears started to flow again.

"She appears to be hemorrhaging. We've taken steps to stop it, but we don't know the cause or if there will be any brain damage. Once we've stopped the bleeding, we'll be able to make more diagnostic tests."

He was calm and reassuring, but his words terrified me. *Bleeding. Brain damage.*

"Please, Mrs. Brown, let's be optimistic." He looked at my mother. "If Mr. Brown were here—"

I shook my head. "He'll be back at the end of the week," Mother said.

"Well," the doctor said, "we'll see if we can get the baby through this critical period."

Dr. Cole left us. My mother and I looked at each other. In the day and a half since Karen's condition became known, Mother hadn't left my side. She murmured encouragement, spooned liquids into me, and answered phone calls from friends and relatives. She'd never seemed a pillar of strength to me. She hadn't coped with her own tragedies: the death of my father, ill health, financial problems. So, seeing her beside me—stoic, calm, helpful (but suffering with me)— was almost a miracle. She found a strength I never knew she had, and it sustained the two of us through the nightmarish days ahead.

Richard called each evening. I could hear his eager voice as he talked to Mother. I couldn't bear to speak to him.

"How are you? How does the case look?" My mother was

almost too cheerful. "Karen? She's fine. Helene's out of the room just now. She didn't expect you to call this early."

We carried out the pretense that Karen was fine through the whole week he was gone, never knowing if she would even be alive the next day.

"Honey," he said when I couldn't avoid speaking to him on the phone, "I've been wanting to hear your voice. How's our little girl?"

I choked back sobs. "She's just fine."

"My father bought cigars with pink bands and Karen's name on them. To give out at the office when I get back."

"Hurry back," I said, struggling to get through the conversation. "I need you."

"It should be Thursday," he said. "I think we'll lose the case, but I don't care. I just want to get back to you and the baby. And I'm bringing my parents."

"Come straight to the hospital, whatever time you get in. Don't wait for visiting hours." I said. "The hospital will let you in at any hour because you've been away all week."

Richard and his parents and the pink-banded cigars arrived five days after my ordeal had begun. They burst into the room, prepared for a joyous reunion. I couldn't hold back my tears. He was beside me, holding me close, as I blurted out the whole story. We all cried then. We all sobbed out the overwhelming grief that little Karen had brought us.

The dream was gone. I was going home, a new mother without her baby. My husband and I were two sad, confused people, with hope halfheartedly promised us by doctors and yet with no hope at all. We had an empty yellow crib and more rosebud kimonos than any baby would ever need. But we had no baby.

Was I a different girl from the one who had decided a little more than a year earlier to marry this man and no other? I was a person suddenly faced with a genuine crisis, but as the tragedy was played out around me, I waited for some miracle to happen. I had already done what I was supposed to do, but life was not conforming to the pattern. I still had my trust and innocence that believed things would be set right.

Chapter 5

ℰ

I'LL HAVE TO tell them at the office that the baby is sick. I won't give out the cigars."

The first day home was agony. Richard and I were two near-strangers thrown together to face a tragedy that would have taxed the most united couple. We had never talked and planned together, and now events had made it almost impossible to start. We clung to each other wordlessly, too numb to think about what was happening to Karen and us.

"I want to go to the hospital and see her," I said.

"We don't think you should, not until she's able to come home. Because . . ."

He couldn't bring himself to say that he and my mother, the doctors, and everyone, didn't want me to go and see a child who might die at any moment. I was a little girl myself, after all, and they knew what was best for me.

I sat in the apartment day after day. I cried while neighbors came and sat with me. I called the doctor every day.

"She might be able to come home soon," I was told. "We're doing more tests."

"She spent a good night. We've controlled the hemorrhaging. Her convulsions seem to be easing."

I lived from day to day, trying to believe that she would soon be with us. I tried not to imagine what harm might have come to her.

A week after I came home, I saw Richard coming up the walk in the early afternoon. I knew that something terrible had happened.

Gently he said: "Try not to get too upset. The baby won't be coming home for a while. We're moving her to another hospital tomorrow for tests."

My tears started again: another agonizing disappointment.

"They can't control her convulsions. The doctors think she should be moved to a place where she'll get more help. But it won't be long before she comes home."

I wanted desperately to believe him. I couldn't have survived if I had thought otherwise.

Richard and his aunt moved the baby from one hospital to the other. I waited at home that long day, alone. After waiting five hours for Karen to be admitted to the hospital, Richard came home stricken by the experience, silent.

The news never got better. The doctors postponed her homecoming week after week. She lost weight. One test followed another; one specialist and then another saw her.

My thin thread of hope that it was all going to work out

snapped the afternoon Richard came home early with my mother.

"The doctors said today that Karen can't ever come home. She is hopelessly damaged."

All my hope died with Richard's words.

"She'll never have any kind of life; she probably won't live longer than a year." Richard was holding back tears. "We'll have to find an institution for her."

I went through the motions of finding a place for Karen, never quite believing that this was really happening to me. We found a nursery that cared for infants who were not expected to live beyond their third year. It had tiny bassinets and flowered curtains and sleeping babies, and it would cost a great deal of money. We made arrangements for Karen to go there when she left the hospital, not knowing how we would pay for it. Already her birth and illness had cost us every penny we had and more.

At home we couldn't discuss Karen. Richard seemed brave and strong. Unknown to me, he and my mother visited Karen at the hospital almost every day. But between us, there was only grief-stricken silence. No one wanted to talk about Karen; no one offered comfort and advice. The specialists were aloof and matter-of-fact. My mother and husband were as overcome as I was. My neighbors—most of them pregnant or new mothers themselves—only brought home to me my loss. I turned at last to the doctor who had delivered Karen and who supplied my only comfort.

"Have another baby as soon as possible," he told me.

"But maybe, just maybe, Karen will come home, and she'll need me."

"Please listen to the experts," he said. "Be brave and strong. You're a perfectly healthy young woman, and there's no reason why you can't have a dozen more children. Let this child go."

I couldn't give up my desperate hope that she would turn out to be perfect and well. I couldn't make the idea of another baby seem like a reality. Only Karen was real, even though I hadn't seen her since she was born.

"You would be ruining your life and your marriage if you tried to bring her home," the doctor said. "Right now she needs constant supervision and medication, and if she survives, there's no telling what she'll be like. Put her out of your mind."

"At least let me see her."

"There's nothing you can do for her. You'd only be breaking your heart."

"She must need her mother. Babies need their mothers."

"She doesn't know the difference, believe me. The best thing to do is forget her."

Wouldn't it have been wonderful—to be able to forget her? If I could have done that, it might have been best, but I was haunted by the memory of her, the child of my dreams, the only two times I had ever seen her: first perfect and beautiful, then red and convulsed, through the window of the hospital nursery.

I tried to forget, but I couldn't.

I wanted a baby so much. Richard and I both did.

Have another baby, the doctor had said. It never occurred to me that the same thing might happen with a second child. I never thought, as many friends and relatives did, that the doctor was somehow responsible for Karen. I never thought—like others—that there was something "wrong" with me or Richard that caused her illness. I never placed the blame on anyone, and no one was ever able to assign any blame. It was enough for me to deal with the fact of her existence, whatever the reasons.

Three months after Karen was born, I was pregnant again. It didn't cancel out the tragedy of Karen, but it gave me a new lease on life. She was still in the hospital. She was going to die eventually. But I was going to have another baby.

One afternoon when I was about two months pregnant, my husband called and said: "Karen has pneumonia. A temperature of 106. She may not live through tomorrow."

This is it, I thought, but it wasn't. She didn't die. Not only did she live through the pneumonia, but she began to improve. Her convulsions stopped; she had only a slight tic in one cheek. I forbade myself to hope. She was going to die, if not now, then later. I had been told this. I had put aside my dreams that Karen would come home to me.

"Mrs. Brown, why haven't you been to see your baby?" A few words to revive a dream I had laid to rest.

It was a specialist in pediatric neurology who had just seen Karen for the first time, calling me from the hospital, demanding to know why I had apparently abandoned my child.

"No one will let me see her. She's going to die."

"No, she isn't. We have changed our diagnosis. If you had been seeing her right along, you would have observed, as we did, that she is raising herself up on her hands like a normal baby."

He talked about reactions, responses, and tests, but I scarcely listened. All I could hear were his words, "We want you to come in here right away."

The miracle had happened. Karen was going to be well. A wonderful, intelligent, learned doctor had just told me so. He wouldn't give me that kind of hope if there were none.

Richard, my mother, and the obstetrician begged me not to set my hopes on what this doctor had said. They argued that other doctors said different things about Karen. I didn't listen to them because I didn't want to hear them. I listened to the neurologist because it seemed to me that holding Karen in my arms would be the best thing that could ever happen to me.

Then someone put my baby in my arms for the second time in her life.

"She's going to be fine, Mrs. Brown." The doctor who had made my dreams come true was just what I wanted him to be: kind and wise, someone who could see beyond the present to a future where my daughter grew healthy and strong.

"She may have a slight limp when she grows up. We can't be certain about that until she's walking. You're going to be very proud of her," he told me, and I believed him without hesitation. I believed him so much that the truth, when it became apparent, made his words seem like the most devastating betrayal of my youth and trust in him.

"Come every day," he told me. "Feed her, hold her, take care of her. She needs you, you'll help her grow stronger."

I was with her every moment from then on. I held her and bathed her and fed her, sustained by the doctor's words, the hope he had given me. For a few weeks she was quiet and unaware of me, but I could see that she was getting stronger. She looked like a normal baby. There were no convulsions. She was like a little doll.

"You're going to be very proud of her." The doctor, repeating his assurances, had disappeared into the lofty recesses of the medical profession, leaving me with lesser practitioners who echoed his words.

I waited to be proud of her, confident that I would be. Then one morning I bent over her crib. Karen was lying quietly as usual. Suddenly she turned her head and saw me, and her eyes gleamed in recognition. She knew me, the person who bathed and fed her. Her mother. It was the beginning of Karen Brown's life and mine.

Chapter 6

૪

W HAT DO YOU plan to do with that child?"

I looked up in surprise at the young woman resident who stopped beside Karen's crib.

"I'm going to take her home. She should weigh enough in a few weeks." Karen was rapidly approaching nine and a half pounds; then, the doctors told me, I would be able to take her home.

"Mrs. Brown," the resident said, "you're making a mistake. This child will be a vegetable. If you spend the rest of your life taking care of her, she'll never recognize you."

I knew that already Karen recognized me when I appeared beside her crib.

"You're wrong, Doctor. Karen knows me now."

She shook her head. I hated her patronizing smile. It was so different from the kindly, fatherly attitude of the specialist. "Your child is permanently damaged. No matter what you believe, no matter what you've been told, she will be totally incapacitated."

"But the neurologist said—"

"Doctors aren't always right, Mrs. Brown. But I can assure you that you will save yourself a lifetime of anguish if you give her up now. I myself wouldn't hold out any hope for your daughter." She shrugged. "It's your decision, but you should be prepared for the worst."

Never! I thought to myself as the resident walked away. The worst was not possible. An important, distinguished specialist had asked me to come to the hospital. He told me that Karen would be perfectly all right. What was a slight limp compared to the joy of having my baby with me to care for and dress up and raise?

A day or two later Karen smiled—a big, toothless grin.

Karen really is going to be all right, I told myself, overcome by the happiness I felt as I watched her gurgle and smile and behave just the way she should.

I look back on that day in disbelief. How much our lives are at the mercy of others, of their diagnoses, their opinions, their statements which, once uttered, come back to haunt us and not them.

I believed what I wanted to believe. I didn't want to have to reach the conclusion that a reasoned consideration of the problem would have required. I didn't want to feel I had to be prepared for the worst; the worst didn't happen to people like me.

My optimistic convictions about Karen were not shared by my family. My husband—worn out by months of grief, of daily visits to the hospital, gloomy news from doctors, his weeping wife—said little. He had struggled through Karen's first desperate months of life as bravely as any man could. My mother had misgivings, but she never openly opposed my decision to bring Karen home.

It was a huge, irrevocable decision for me and my whole family.

If I hadn't gone to Karen and encouraged her to live (and I believe I *did* encourage the spark of life in her), she might have gone to that pretty nursery-hospital for hopeless infants and died there. I might not have forgotten her completely, but the pain would have lessened and perhaps in time would have gone away.

If I had been a middle-aged woman and Karen was my only chance to have a child, it would have been a different kind of decision, with different kinds of expectations for her and me.

But I was a young woman who could expect to have many healthy babies. At my age I didn't have to live the rest of my life with a handicapped child, even if she turned out better than anyone predicted. With all the advice I received, it never penetrated my immature thinking what she was going to mean to my life in the long run.

A person's relationship with a handicapped child is a relationship quite unlike any other. Husbands and wives drift apart and marriages end; healthy children grow from dependence to adulthood and independence and eventually leave their parents; parents themselves grow old and die. But a handicapped child is with you from birth—forever. He or she is a responsibility that always hovers at the edge of your life.

Seven years after Karen was born, I was beginning to understand. Seven long, hard years later, I went back to the neurologist who had told me to love her and take her home.

"Do you remember me, Doctor?" I asked. He did not. "Don't you remember that you told me my child who had had a brain hemorrhage and convulsions from birth would be all right, that she would have only a slight limp, and I would be proud of her when she was grown up?"

The doctor listened, impatient for me to leave.

"You told me to come to the hospital and take her home. Now my marriage is falling apart and my little boy is suffering."

The doctor was indifferent to my tears. He tapped a pencil on his desk.

"I can't handle her. I don't know what to do. She's not all right. She's all wrong. You told me to love her, and that she would be just fine. But she's not fine. What should I do?"

I knew almost before he said it: "Put her in an institution."

He went back to the work on his desk. He was finished with me and Karen.

I had not had the slightest glimpse of this kind of future when I finally brought Karen home in the early spring. She was nearly seven months old, and I had nothing but hope for her.

The neighbors who had sat with me through the days when Karen was hovering between life and death flocked to the apartment to see my remarkable baby who had survived. Grandmothers, aunts, and uncles cuddled her and loved her, and she gurgled and giggled and grew healthier and prettier. She was the baby of my dreams after all.

We watched Karen closely in the months that followed her homecoming. We took her to doctors who all differed in their diagnoses. She was a perfect-looking baby with a pretty body. She had no physical deformity that I could see.

(37)

My son, David, was born a year after Karen. The same doctor delivered him, and he was handsome and healthy.

Karen and David were almost like twins. I fed the two of them together and bathed them together. They slept side by side in twin cribs in the bedroom, while Richard and I slept on a convertible sofa in the living room. There was no way, in our innocence and happiness, that Richard and I could foresee the problems of the future. For us, the dream that had been postponed by those first desperate months of Karen's life had finally come true. It was some time before we knew how incapacitated Karen was going to be.

We sought reassurance from doctors, confirmation of the promise that she would be all right. They spoke to us about cerebral palsy, physical limitations, poor attention span, a possible hearing defect, even mental retardation; but no one, I concluded, really knew, so I blocked out the most terrible possibilities from my mind.

I so enjoyed watching her react to the world in her way. Didn't that prove that somehow, in some way, she was all right? She lay in her crib and watched the mobile suspended over it. She gurgled and reached up to it. I saw her tiny hands move, but her fingers didn't seem to work properly. At feeding time it was Karen who was held and fed because she couldn't grasp her bottle. David had a bottle holder.

When David cried in the night he didn't wake her. It was beginning to dawn on us that she might be deaf.

Soon I was telling Richard that David was starting to walk. Karen, a full year older, was the same as when I brought her home: plump and healthy-looking, but unable to sit up or crawl or feed herself.

Now I knew that there was something desperately wrong with her, that it wasn't going to be just a slight limp.

And knowing this, I still managed to pretend a lot. I dressed the two children in brother-and-sister outfits and wheeled them around the neighborhood in a double stroller. Our home was filled with friends and relatives, ready to hug and kiss my children. Mother, who lived nearby, saw them every day. She brought gifts and loved them. She was also our constant babysitter. (Did I understand then that she was our sitter because I couldn't bring myself to leave Karen with a stranger?)

"Richard, what are we going to do about Karen?"

He had no answer. Perhaps he never even asked himself the question. My husband was kind and loving and hard-working. He was willing to do the dishes and empty the diaper pail. He fussed over Karen and played with David. But he didn't seem to be worried the way I was, constantly now, as I watched her not becoming what she was supposed to be.

It was then that I began to feel that I was losing whatever grip I had on my marriage. In those first three years a gulf grew between us almost unnoticed because of the problems of our daily life.

"My dear woman," a doctor said to me years later when my marriage had broken up, "you never had a chance. What chance, really, did you have with your marriage? In those first years of pregnancies and troubles, how could either of you have grown and adjusted?"

Years later I could answer: "Yes, you're right. There was no way. The man I married when I was only a child myself was never, through any fault of his own, the man I wanted him to be, and after Karen was born, he withdrew even more. He was more willing to let things happen to him than to make things happen."

But at twenty-two, after only three years of marriage, I hadn't the understanding to see the pattern of our lives.

I could only see the immediate situation, and I took stock.

Karen smiles a lot. That's nice.

She's a beautiful child with blond, corkscrew curls and luminous, green eyes. A Shirley Temple doll. But she can't sit up. She can't crawl. She's not toilet-trained and may never be. She doesn't seem to be able to hear. She can't talk.

My husband goes to work and gives me his paycheck. He helps around the house and is affectionate with me, and devoted to our children. But he has no interest in going out and socializing; his home and his job are his life. He's willing to ignore the problem of Karen and see what the next day brings. And we don't talk about the really important things in our life.

David is growing up to be sensitive and serious and self-reliant—a normal, healthy boy. What will his future be, with a sister like his? Is he going to have to grow up with a handicapped person, until the day he leaves home?

And me. Was I going to be a perpetual nursemaid to a perpetual infant? Where was the romance and excitement of life, of marriage, the two people in tune, living as one?

It seemed to me that all of that was finished before it had begun. I had none of the nice things I wanted. What I had were responsibilities, and most of all, Karen.

Karen was at the bottom of every problem, every question I asked myself.

I had no plans for working, for a career, for anything beyond my home and marriage and family, but there was something wrong with each one of those things.

Karen was three. I looked at her and said to myself: Enough. Enough babies and struggling to raise Karen and David. Enough long silences that stretch through the evenings, with my husband reading the paper or watching television, when we have so very much to talk about.

The one thing Karen's doctors seemed able to agree on was that she had cerebral palsy. There was no cure, I knew, but there had to be help. What did other parents with handicapped children do?

I looked up the telephone number of United Cerebral Palsy.

"I have a little girl," I said to the woman who answered at the Cerebral Palsy Center. "She's three and she has cerebral palsy. Can I bring her to you?"

I could bring her at once.

Chapter 7

ꙮ

A NEW DRESS, hair curled, tiny white shoes and socks trimmed with lace, ruffled panties over her diapers, Karen looked like a beautiful rag doll. The people at the Cerebral Palsy Center were enchanted with the pretty puppet I brought them.

"We have several programs," Mrs. King, the head of the center, told me. "We can certainly fit Karen into one of them."

Suddenly Karen was taken out of my life for three half-days a week. For the first time in three years, I had a breathing spell, time to think about myself. As soon as she was gone, I realized what a burden she had become. And as soon as I realized that, I felt guilty. Just as quickly, I tried to put it out of my mind. The center would be good for her.

At the center no one knew quite what to do with her. She wasn't like the other children. At first glance, she looked so well, but she obviously wasn't. No conclusive testing of her hearing and intelligence had yet been done, although it was apparent that she was handicapped in these areas as well as physically.

"Karen is a challenge," Mrs. King told me. "I can't give you any satisfactory answers about her yet. Her hearing is certainly impaired. We'll do our best for her."

Two decades ago, what people knew about dealing with cerebral palsy victims, what they could offer children like Karen, was limited. In our center, mostly inexperienced volunteers—parents like Richard and me—tried to keep the children occupied and to teach them what we could. It wasn't a coordinated program with a proven record of progress; it was an attempt by desperate parents to ease the tragedy of their lives, to find some help for their children. In a single class there were muscular dystrophy children, autistic children, all levels of retardation, as well as children with a wide range of disabilities under the heading of *cerebral palsy*. After an initial awakening, Karen, of course, gained less and less from classroom situations. A deaf child with limited attention span and severe physical disabilities couldn't be expected to sit still and learn colors and numbers.

There was no other facility for her, and I was grateful for what I had. In the years since Karen attended classes at the center, however, there hasn't been much progress in dealing with multiply handicapped children. Only a handful of the schools that I have seen as I traveled across the country have the broad range of facilities to treat children like Karen and provide meaningful educational and training programs, and even when they do, the cost is almost invariably beyond the means of all but the wealthy.

If Karen failed to learn much intellectually at the Cerebral Palsy Center, I still had hopes that physical therapy might benefit her.

"Mrs. Brown," I was told first, "we think you should get Karen a wheelchair." Karen got a wheelchair at three and a half. She could turn the wheels with the palms of her hands and propel herself around.

Next it was decided that she should be fitted for leg braces. At four and a half she had heavy braces that extended from her waist to her feet. She was able to stand a little and walk with the aid of parallel bars, but the weight of the braces was almost too much for her.

Advice came rapidly from all directions: "Mrs. Brown, Karen is managing to crawl now. Someday she should be able to learn to walk properly." "Mrs. Brown, I'm afraid Karen will never be able to walk unaided." "Karen would benefit from intensive physical therapy." "Physical therapy would be of no value in Karen's case."

I wanted to shut my ears to all the conflicting statements from doctors, therapists, experts in cerebral palsy, and just wait to see what happened, but it would have been too easy, and it wouldn't have been right. I kept on hoping, and we kept on taking her to whomever we thought might be able to help her.

After Karen's first couple of years at the center with little or nothing to show for it, I began trying to make my husband see how little she was being helped. "The most we can say is that she's out of the house for a few mornings a week. Richard, there has to be more to our life than this."

I had had an opportunity to observe the other mothers who did volunteer work at the center. They seemed to believe that a life of total self-sacrifice for their handicapped children was the only possibility. I didn't want that for us. We were too young, there was too much ahead of us. Richard didn't seem to want to notice, or perhaps he found their attitude acceptable. I did not. It doesn't have to be that way, I wanted to scream at those mothers and at him. Life doesn't have to be budget dinners and shabby housedresses and total acceptance of everything that's bad.

I wasn't going to be overcome by my child. We were both going to have lives of our own. David was going to have a life. My husband could have a life if he wanted it. I was already living in a future in which I was liberated from the tyranny of a kind of motherhood I had never expected and did not want. Once again I had decided how things were supposed to be; I was fighting another losing battle to make reality conform with my ideal.

I rejected self-sacrifice without realizing that I had committed myself to another kind of self-sacrifice. The continuing deep, deep guilt about Karen shaped my life for years and compelled me to become someone I never dreamed of being. It forced me to destroy—in atonement for her—whatever happiness my life brought me.

I asked my husband for a divorce. No longer was I merely frustrated by him. He enraged me. I was twenty-four years old, and I felt so sorry for myself and so disappointed in my husband for what I considered his failure to deal constructively with Karen, his inability to fulfill my romantic dreams, that I wanted out of my marriage under any circumstances. I would move with my two children into Mother's one-bedroom apartment, back to the life I had tried to escape by marrying him, just to be free of him.

But he begged and pleaded, and I stayed.

Only once did my mother say to me: "Well, what do you

want? You have a husband who loves you. He has a steady job. He's home every night. He's devoted to you and the children. There are a lot of women worse off than you."

She was right, of course, according to her terms, which were the terms in which most of society viewed marital relationships then.

Was there something wrong with me, I wondered, that I wanted something more: plans, dreams, mutual goals, being intuitive about each other's feelings and needs, surprise, excitement. It was never there for me in my marriage, and I was too immature to realize that you don't magically transform the person you've married into a closer approximation of an ideal.

Besides, came the suggestion from all sides, you have this handicapped child to worry about. You'd better hang onto your husband. You're lucky to have someone who'll stick by you.

The idea haunted me for years, long after my husband and I were separated. Because of my child, I was lucky to have any man interested in me. I should be grateful for anyone, never mind whether he was right for me. I stayed with my husband then because I still had no justification for leaving him that I could give to people; the opinion of others was important enough to me to feel I needed a justification. But I knew that eventually I would leave, so instead of trying to make the marriage work, I planned how to end it.

In order to leave my husband and provide Karen with some kind of life, I had to be in a position to care for her and David and me financially. I had an inkling of my future obligations to her: we were probably going to grow old together. Everything I planned depended on finding work that would bring me an income large enough to live on, if and when the time came. (Richard, I believed, wasn't motivated to make the kind of money Karen would need.) This was an enormous step for someone who had lived her life on the assumption that a man—a father, a husband—was going to take care of her.

I had no work background to speak of: three months as a lovesick typist in a clerical pool was hardly a foundation on which to build the next forty or fifty years of my life. I had studied fine arts but not in terms of a career. I had a love of beauty and comfortable living inherited from my mother, but my present circumstances didn't remotely resemble those of my childhood years. Compared to us, my friends and neighbors seemed well off. They had nicely furnished apartments and one child to our two. They didn't have our medical bills. We were constantly having Karen seen by yet another doctor. I envied my neighbors' new furniture, their carpets and china, all the touches we simply didn't have money for, the things which, to me, represented a happy home.

Grandma Sara, in her wisdom, had given me a sewing machine for a wedding present, doubtless with the thought of me bent over the machine running up elegant outfits for myself and ruffles and frills for her future great-grandchildren. Since I didn't know how to sew, the sewing machine stood idle in a corner of the bedroom for the first couple of years of my married life.

My neighbors' cafe curtains with their ball fringe finally drove me to the sewing machine. I was going to have living room draperies that were the best thing our neighborhood had ever seen. I was going to have bedspreads and dust ruffles and cafe curtains of my own to fill my empty windows. The granddaughter of the Czarina's seamstress was not going to be outdone by a bunch of suburban women who could afford to shop at B. Altman's.

I sorted through every home decorating magazine I could lay my hands on, cutting out pictures of rooms I liked and color schemes and drapery designs, until I could close my eyes and see our three-room apartment look like a magazine spread. Then I scrounged and saved until I had fifty dollars, which I took to a remnant store and invested in fabric.

When the apartment was finished, I couldn't quite believe what I had done. It was special; it was beautiful. In a life that hadn't had too many glorious moments, it was a triumph.

Women friends began stopping in for advice about decorating their apartments and something clicked. If I knew how to do this kind of work and people liked what I did, maybe it was the key to my future and Karen's. On the other hand, I had a suspicion that it was one thing to go to a department store with a girl friend to pick out bedspreads and quite another to set myself up as an interior decorator and expect to be paid for it. There had to be a way to bridge the gap between amateur and professional.

I called a design school in New York City to find out if it offered evening courses. Yes, I was told, the school had an evening program that took three years, three nights a week. By juggling household accounts, I could just afford the fees. I knew I was going to that school and learn to be a decorator. That night when Richard came home from work, I said: "I've signed up to go to school at night. I start the day after tomorrow."

Even in a day when it was fairly uncommon for young wives to go back to school, he didn't ask any questions. He didn't ask how I was going to do it or why. All he knew was that two days later when he came home, his dinner was ready, the children were bathed and fed and in their cribs, and I was putting on my coat.

"I start school tonight," I said. "I'll be back at nine-thirty. Dinner is in the oven."

I got into our old gray Plymouth and drove from Long Island to Manhattan, to a new life and new world. Suddenly I was in the middle of Manhattan three nights a week, sitting in a classroom with people who were not suburban housewives. No one knew about Karen or my unhappy home; I had no excuses to make for the glaring imperfections of my life.

I fell wholeheartedly into the escape that school offered, not realizing that it was as much an escape as it was an opportunity to learn about something I loved. For three years I lived for those school nights. Days were filled with fetching and carrying Karen to and from the Cerebral Palsy Center, with attending to whatever therapy was recommended at the moment (hours of backbreaking exercises with her, hours of heartbreaking efforts to teach her something, anything), with meeting the demands of my active young son, with keeping house, with all the details of daily living. I was a dutiful, devoted housewife. I would have been shocked then to be told that my homework and scrapbooks and research in libraries were shaping a different kind of life for me.

Quietly, easily, I began to move into a new place in life. Interior design was the profession I wanted. What I didn't think about was what it meant to have a profession. I didn't want to consider the fundamental conflict between marriage and career that was almost inevitable for women in the late 1950s. I blocked out the personal conflicts between my youthful dreams of perfection in love and marriage and my need to be—what? A star? The object of admiration by whom? My husband? My children? My neighbors?

I began to get clients, people who hired me and paid me.

Mastery of my profession gave me the sense of *not* being at the mercy of an unfortunate set of circumstances. I felt strong, because in one area of my life I had some control over what I was doing. I clearly had no control over my marriage; it merely drifted along. I had no control over Karen, who continued at the Cerebral Palsy Center but who was getting no better and in fact was becoming increasingly disruptive. David, in nursery school, was living in the shadow of his handicapped sister. I was powerless, through ignorance and uncertainty, to know how I could keep him from being damaged by the life we had handed him.

I have no clear image of myself during those years. I was struggling, mostly alone, to find solutions for myself and my family. I raged at the marriage that failed to satisfy me and longed to be free. For what, I didn't know. Not to be myself, because I didn't know who I was. To be free of Karen was unthinkable. Even then, I understood that she was going to be with me for the rest of my life —or hers. Freedom from my husband, possibly. The thought of divorce came easily to me, but that was an admission that most of my adult life so far had been based on a mistake. I wasn't ready for that.

Helene is just too overpowering for Richard. People were quick to blame the obvious. They saw me doing so many things—decorating, being a mother, wearing the kind of clothes I knew I had to have to be part of my outside world. It wasn't that I was too much for him. I was too different. We were locked into a marriage where he preserved his sanity by silence and I preserved mine by doing things.

Karen, always Karen, at the center of our problems.

I was determined that I wasn't going to be overcome by Karen, nor was David. Total innocence is tarnished eventually. The curtain is drawn aside, and the desperate rush to perpetuate a prettiness that doesn't exist is halted by simple facts of life: I had a handicapped child who wasn't so nice to be around. I had a husband who wasn't, after all, the man of my dreams. I had a son who couldn't help but be hurt by the turmoil created by his parents and his sister.

I had to choose between what might be fruitless self-sacrifice to the demands of my life or attempt to reconstruct the circumstances completely, to make new paths for all of us.

Chapter 8

❦

A YEAR OR SO AGO, I took Karen to meet a group of handicapped children and adults being picked up for a summer camp. It had been a terrible year in both our lives. In the days I had just lived through, beset with personal and professional problems and barely coping with a shattered mental state, I had often wondered if I had done the right thing for Karen in her growing-up years. Had it really been right for me to divide myself between a demanding career, which I loved, and raising Karen to be as nearly a whole person as possible, in spite of her devastating handicaps? Maybe I should have devoted myself entirely to her all those years, kept her with me. True, she had made great progress since she was a child, thanks to the schools I had sent her to. True, I was successful in my profession. But I was also depressed, defeated, uncertain, unhappy. I had been through a period that had left me feeling guiltier than ever about her and the choices I had made. Would another way have been better for both of us?

On that Saturday morning I watched Karen stumbling awkwardly among the trunks and suitcases, roaming about meeting people, falling down and getting up.

"What are you doing?" I asked her in sign language when I caught her eye. "You can't walk around here. There are too many people."

She laughed and started out again. She fell and looked at me to come and pick her up.

"No," I said. "I'm not picking you up. You get yourself up."

One more pleading look, in case I wasn't serious; then she knew she'd lost. She got herself to her feet.

"Now stand here beside me and be quiet." The bus to the camp was due in a few minutes.

I was irritable in the June heat. Downcast, Karen stood beside me, sneaking looks at the new people arriving, eager to venture out again to greet them, having no language but friendliness and no mobility except her lumbering walk that took her from place to place, though not very well.

A battered old car pulled up in front of us, and I had an answer to all my questions and doubts about what I had done with our lives.

A man got out of the car and took a shabby wheelchair from the trunk. A woman opened the other door. With a shock I recognized her as the mother of a little girl at the Cerebral Palsy Center nearly fifteen years before.

Alice and Karen had been five-year-olds in wheelchairs. No one held out much hope for Karen, but Alice, they said, had a good chance for an almost normal life with proper treatment. She had none of Karen's retardation or hearing problems. Her physical disabilities might be overcome with therapy. Yet here was Alice being lifted from the car by her father and put in a wheelchair. Her mother, whom I remembered as a cheerful young woman devoted to her daughter, was grayhaired and tired-looking. It was only with difficulty that I recognized Alice. The sight of her now revealed what her life had been like since the center. She had stayed at home, cared for by loving parents who had catered to her handicap. She had been sitting in her wheelchair for fifteen years, growing overweight from lack of exercise, becoming more incapacitated as the years went by. She wasn't a young woman of twenty, the way Karen was. She was an old woman. All three of them were old, defeated human beings.

Karen, the child no one had any hope for, was lost momentarily in the crowd. I caught a glimpse of her, laughing and happy. As she came back toward me, she stopped beside Alice's wheelchair, puzzled, then recognized her friend from years before. She squealed delightedly and put her arms around Alice's neck and kissed her, before tumbling down the street into my arms to tell me about her latest adventure.

I could have been like those parents, I kept thinking to myself—prematurely old and broken by life. Karen would have been like Alice, bound to her wheelchair, quiet and sullen. Perhaps they were content with what they had done with their lives. At least they had survived as a family. But survival alone had never been enough for me. For all the bad things that had happened, there were so many good things, not the least of which was that Karen was grown up and bursting with health and vitality, David was grown up stable and healthy, and I, at last was beginning to grow up and face the demons that had haunted me all my life.

What was right for me was not necessarily right for everyone. For some, keeping a handicapped child at home is the best solution, but for others it is not. Seeing Alice, her parents, and Karen, I knew that the tremendous effort involved in planning and working and deciding what was best had been worth it.

As it was, I began slowly, without guidance or advice.

When Karen was about five the cerebral palsy people suggested that she be put in a rehabilitation center. She needed more therapy and instruction than they could provide.

We took Karen to Bird S. Coler Hospital on Welfare Island. The hospital treats both geriatric cases and children with physical disabilities. They kept her for four months for a complete evaluation. She had hearing, physical therapy, and IQ tests. She was fitted for new braces weighing more than she herself weighed. They gave her a hearing aid that she didn't know what to do with, because it didn't help her to hear. When I visited her, I found her sitting in her wheelchair, wearing her braces and hearing aid. The wheels of the chair were tied so she couldn't move anywhere; there was no one to look after her. When she wanted attention, she pulled the hearing aid from her ear and bit it until someone noticed and came to fuss over her. It was disheartening.

At the end of four months we were summoned to the hospital for a verdict. We sat in a conference room while the doctors filed in with their manila folders marked "Karen Brown" and read their reports.

"Your daughter is a hopeless case."

"She is severely retarded. Her intelligence tests show a very low IQ. Learning possibilities are minimal."

"She has nerve deafness. We doubt that any device or

therapy can help her hearing problem. She will never learn to talk."

"We don't believe that physical therapy will help her."

"She might be able to walk with braces, but only with difficulty."

"If you cannot keep her at home, we recommend that you place her permanently in a state institution."

The doctors gathered up their folders and quietly removed themselves from the room, while Richard and I gathered up our bitter disappointment, along with Karen, wheelchair, braces, and hearing aid and drove home silently. My husband had a grim, tight-lipped expression on his face that was becoming familiar to me.

Karen had been returned to us essentially unchanged after four months in the one rehabilitation center that might have helped her. Any hope we had had for her was gone.

I couldn't fault the rehabilitation center for its diagnosis. Karen did appear to be very low-functioning. Because of that and her deafness, she was unmotivated to do anything or learn anything. Her whole life centered on using people for her comfort. She craved and sought attention and affection. It was almost as if she got up every day just to see how many people she could get to wait on her, hold her, be next to her.

She learned to crawl when she was about two and crawled for the better part of eight years. She learned to climb the sides of her crib and playpen to attract attention. It seemed to me that her desire to get from one place to another indicated some intelligence, more than the doctors credited her with. A vegetable doesn't want to get from here to there; it is content to stay where it is. But beyond this, I had to admit that Karen was an eternal baby who wanted only to be held and loved. She knew who belonged to her, who would hold her, who would come running. She laughed when she was happy and cried when someone went against her desires.

After the rehabilitation center Karen was taken back into the cerebral palsy program with some reluctance. If they didn't know how to deal with her at the beginning, certainly at five or six or seven, she would fit in even less. She was a robust, healthy little girl, increasingly demanding, heavy, difficult to move around.

I seemed to be constantly lifting her and her heavy braces. I dressed her in the morning and put on her braces. I lifted her into her wheelchair and lifted her out into the car that took her to school. She was back in the afternoon to be lifted out, to be undressed and bathed, to be put in the wheelchair and then to bed. There was cooking and cleaning for the rest of the family—the laundry, the dishes, shopping. Attending to my decorating work and paying attention to David. David was adrift. He was never left out, but somehow attention was always riveted on Karen. One day David picked up a spoon for the first time and started eating by himself, but I can't recall that anyone remarked about it. At six or seven, Karen made her first attempt to eat by herself, and the next day, my mother, mother-in-law, cousins, and aunts were at our house to see this marvel and praise her. David's father was affectionate, but there were no bike-riding lessons or fishing trips or expeditions to baseball games. David's outings to zoos and parks were with his Grandmother Esther. I worried about what this life was doing to him.

It crept up on me, but gradually I had to face what I feared the most. To save all four of us, I was going to have to send Karen away.

Mealtimes were becoming a horror. If no one was paying attention to her, Karen pulled everything in reach off the table and laughed. She screamed with rage if she was taken from the room. She displayed a kind of animal cunning in devising ways to disrupt the household: taking David's toys, following me about on hands and knees, and so on. David displayed a remarkable patience for a little boy; from the time they were both very small, he seemed to sense that his sister was different.

Karen was a wild, untrained, apparently untrainable, little creature.

I loved her desperately. It had been such a struggle to raise her at all, but she wasn't getting any better. She was growing worse, harder to handle each day. I loved her, but at the same time, I resented her. I was trapped in my unhappy home. I couldn't help but notice, when I was out with my clients, that no one else seemed to live under such desperate circumstances. I saw women with homes in which there was laughter and children coming and going. They had time to relax, time for themselves. No lives are perfect, but it came home to me again and again how far from the happy household I had dreamed of our existence was. I plunged into a deep depression.

The social worker at the Cerebral Palsy Center called us in for a parents' conference. Karen had been back at the center after her stay at Bird S. Coler for some time, but she wasn't getting along well. We had been through years of sitting in doctors' offices and clinics, waiting for still another diagnosis of Karen, and I had come to dread these conferences.

"I believe Mrs. King has spoken to you from time to time in the past few months about Karen's classroom behavior."

I nodded numbly to the social worker.

"She's become so disruptive that she's hindering the other children, who want to learn. Of course, we know that since she can't hear, she can't be expected to participate fully."

The social worker shrugged. "We just don't have any program here tailored to her handicaps."

Richard and I avoided looking at each other.

"I'm afraid the decision is that we can't keep Karen at the center any longer. We'd like you to make other arrangements for her by the end of this term."

I wanted to cry. "Do you have any recommendations?" I said instead.

"Unfortunately, Mrs. Brown, I can't answer that. I don't think there are any day programs in this area that she would benefit from. Of course, there are out-of-town schools you could investigate."

She handed me a copy of *The Directory of Schools for Exceptional Children.*

"Residential schools are likely to cost a lot of money, though. I'd guess your best bet for her would be a state institution."

State institution. It sent a chill through me.

We had looked at a state institution not long before, when we realized that Karen might have to be sent away. The place we visited in upper New York State had acres of beautiful grounds around stately old brick buildings. The director greeted us pleasantly and explained the programs. "We have many multiply handicapped youngsters here," he told us, "and a full program of schooling and therapy. I'll show you the facilities after I show you the building where your daughter would live."

I had heard that groups of eight or ten children lived together in cottages there, and I visualized Karen in such a setting. It wasn't home; it was more like a boarding school.

"Yes," said the director when I mentioned the cottages, "we do have living arrangements like those."

We were walking across the neatly manicured grounds to a large brick building.

"Those facilities are for the ambulatory children only. Since Karen is so severely handicapped, we would have to put her in with our lowest functioning youngsters who need maximum care. This building over here."

He pointed to the building we were headed for. Lulled by the pleasant conversation, I was prepared for nothing.

I had once seen the movie *The Snake Pit*. It was horrifying, but of course it wasn't real; movie reality was the nice stuff—happiness and romance and rose-covered cottages.

When I entered the building where I had been told my child would live, I was in a snake pit far worse than anything on the screen, worse than anything I could have imagined. Half-naked children lay about on the floor of an empty room, unnoticed and uncared for. A broken television set hummed quietly in a corner. The director kept up his smooth conversation as we walked through the room. Richard and I, with clenched teeth, tried not to look at the misery around us, children in their own dirt, severely handicapped boys and girls walking or crawling about, with no attendant in sight.

Never, I promised myself during that agonizing visit; never would my child spend her life here or any place like it. Now I heard the Cerebral Palsy Center's social worker telling me that the one place where I could certainly send her was a state institution. Or keep her at home. A private boarding school seemed a remote possibility. My decorating business brought in some money, but it was irregular. It couldn't be depended on for paying monthly school fees. Richard's income was enough to support the family, but that was all.

I had never felt so alone. No one had any advice to offer. My husband and I were faced with another monumental decision, and he had nothing to say. My mother suffered with me, but she was working to support herself; the problem I faced was beyond the scope of her imagining. She was a loving grandmother, but she wasn't a decision-maker. Nor were my uncles, my inlaws.

Daily I turned over and over in my mind my choices, my guilty reasons, and my fears. I was a quitter to want to send her away. I was a monster to hate her for what she was doing to my life. I was selfish to want to keep her by me when she would be better off in a place where she could have training and therapy, where she would be like the other children. When I lay in bed, crying night after night beside my sleeping husband, I was harming four lives, not just my own.

Yet when I looked at Karen's angelic face, tucked into her bed, I felt I couldn't part with the child I had tended so carefully all these years. She was so helpless, she needed so much love and care. How could I leave her to strangers? She had been the focus of my life for seven years. The cord that bound her to me twisted tighter and tighter around my heart as the months slipped by.

Then I looked at David, a handsome, lively boy who never complained but whose whole future was at stake. My future, the one I had believed in so deeply, seemed irretrievably gone.

I prayed, not knowing to whom or what I was praying. I said aloud: "If you want me to send her away, help me. God, if you are there, and if this is the right thing for me to do, put the strength in me to do it."

The weeks of the Cerebral Palsy Center school term slipped away while I prayed and cried. In my grief and frustration I grew to hate my silent husband, never realizing that he was suffering too. His dreams were broken. It was his child too—and his unhappy marriage.

Then from somewhere I found the strength I needed. I found it in the love I had for my little girl and in the resentment I felt for her and my life. Perhaps my prayers were answered. Wherever it came from, it saved her and me. It freed the family from the bonds of anger and frustration that could only have made our mutual existence worse.

One day I began to look for a school for Karen.

Chapter 9

༃

Aschool close to home—New York, Connecticut, New Jersey, Pennsylvania—and a school with a tuition we could afford. It seemed like an impossible task. Two hundred dollars a month was beyond our means; most schools charged even higher tuitions.

I pored over *The Directory of Schools for Exceptional Children:* day schools, residential schools, schools for orthopedically handicapped children, emotionally disturbed children, mentally retarded, blind, multiply handicapped children; age requirements, length of stay, services, tuition. I was profoundly discouraged. Having made the decision to find a place for Karen, I learned that no place was available. Most schools had specific requirements: must be ambulatory; must be toilet-trained; must be one hundred percent self-help; no deaf children. At seven, Karen wasn't toilet-trained. She couldn't feed or dress herself; she couldn't hear or speak or walk except with parallel bars and wearing braces.

Now and then I came across a school that mentioned no restrictions. Tuition started at seven or eight thousand dollars a year, which was about our gross income.

I would have to get a regular job, I decided, to pay Karen's school tuition, provided we could find a place for her, an inexpensive place.

The listing of Downingtown Special School in Pennsylvania was very brief. It didn't mention any restrictions on the kind of children accepted. As I read through the *Directory* again and again, I kept coming back to that school: the tuition was only a hundred and fifty dollars a month. Surely I could find a job that paid that much. And a place in Pennsylvania couldn't be too far from New York City; I wouldn't be sending Karen to the ends of the earth.

After considerable procrastination (what if all I received from the school was a sharp refusal?) I sat down and wrote a letter in which I told them all about Karen and my problems with her and how badly handicapped she was. I told them that I had a younger child at home and that I couldn't keep her any longer. I practically begged the school to take her.

"Dear Mrs. Brown," came a letter in reply, written in a foreign-looking, spiky handwriting, "we would be happy to accept Karen at our school immediately. We are a small school with only twelve children, ranging in age from six to twelve. They are treated as members of a family and receive individual attention from our staff, who live in the house with them. We have had much success in helping children with a variety of handicaps, and we believe we can help Karen. In future years, we plan to run the school according to a regular school year, with a two-month summer holiday when the children are not in residence, but this year we are keeping the school open during the summer months, and we will be glad to have Karen with us."

"Yes," I wrote back, "I would like to send Karen to your school. We will bring her in June."

June was two months away. I had two months in which to find a job that brought in at least a hundred and fifty dollars a month.

"Richard," I said, handing him the letter from the school, "Karen is going away to this school in June."

He looked at me.

"She has to go, you know," I said. "She has to have help. The Cerebral Palsy Center won't keep her. I can't have her here all day long."

"I know, but I hate the idea of sending her to strangers. She's so little."

Deep inside, he had the same worries and fears for Karen that I had. I felt a new closeness to him. Maybe Karen's going would bring us back together.

"I'm going to get a job to help pay her tuition. I'll find something in the decorating business. There are all those big New York firms that do hotels and offices. We'll work out something so David won't be coming home from school to an empty house."

Hopeful and confident, an interior decorator with several years of experience in my own business, I set out to make the rounds of employment agencies that handled positions with interior design firms in the city.

By the third or fourth interview it dawned on me that the business world was not waiting for a married woman of twenty-seven with two small children. "We don't seem to have anything suitable, Mrs. Brown." "In many ways you're overqualified for the jobs we have." I must have looked odd indeed to people accustomed to seeing twenty-year-old design school graduates.

"We can send you on an interview, but I doubt very much . . . someone with family responsibilities is hard to place . . . most of our placements are rather younger. . . ."

I did what other women did who had reached a certain level in their profession and were without a job: I became a clerk typist.

I found a three-day-a-week job in the public relations department of a large New York hospital. It paid enough to take care of Karen's tuition, and I still had two days a week to devote to decorating when jobs came along.

I had taken two very difficult steps. I had finally committed myself mentally and in fact to sending Karen to school in June, and I couldn't go back on that now; and I had taken a job I hated to make it possible.

The third, and hardest, step was to take Karen to Pennsylvania and put her in their care. We hadn't visited the school before we packed her up in June. I knew I had no choice but to send her there. If I had seen the school first and hadn't liked it, I would have given up the idea of sending her away at all.

We drove from New York to Pennsylvania with Karen and David in terrible early summer heat. "I'm not going to survive this," I kept thinking. "It's like giving my child up for adoption."

"I think we're lost," my husband said. "Try to keep Karen quiet."

Traveling for four and a half hours with Karen was like traveling with a querulous newborn infant in an eight-year-old body. She cried, she fidgeted, she pulled at me and David and her father. We had to stop frequently to feed her, wash her, and change her diapers.

As we made our way through the unfamiliar countryside, we were like four wanderers in the desert. When we drove up to the school, it was as if we had reached an oasis.

"This must be the place," Richard said. It was a fairy-tale house in the middle of beautiful rolling country, an old stone Pennsylvania farmhouse surrounded by fields and hills, flowers and trees.

"Are you sure?" I was afraid we might be in the wrong place. Someone was going to send us down the road to a terrible-looking, bleak institutional building, and I would make Richard turn the car around immediately and go home.

"Go up to the door and find out," he said.

A frail little woman answered my knock.

"I'm looking for Marion McLeod," I said. "I'm Helene Brown, bringing my daughter—"

"I am Miss McLeod," the woman said with a trace of a British accent. "I hope you didn't have any trouble finding us." She took my hand. "We're so glad to have you here."

Her face lit up with a kind of spiritual glow. She turned to Richard, who was holding Karen, all dressed up as usual, so the school would think she was so wonderful that they would keep her for that reason if no other.

"And this is our Karen," she said. "She's extraordinary. She's beautiful."

Moments of true peace come rarely in the lives of parents of handicapped children. I remember those first minutes with Marion McLeod as being the most peaceful in a long time.

"And here is Mr. Brown." She beamed at Richard. "I'm

Miss McLeod, the supervisor here. "And your little boy, how handsome he is. You must come and meet everyone."

Suddenly she turned from us and called out over the fields in a high-pitched, birdlike voice: "Hans, Renata, Ursula, come quickly. See who is here!"

In a scene straight from *The Sound of Music,* a group of ruddy-faced, laughing, smiling young men and women, wearing alpine peasant clothes came bounding in from the fields. With them were beautiful little children, all joyous and healthy-looking. None of the children appeared to be handicapped. They all gathered around us, exclaiming over Karen and hugging me and Richard and David. It was comical, yet touching; everyone seemed genuinely delighted that we were there.

"We must show the house. We must see Karen's room. Renata, get the refreshments ready. Hans, you push Karen's wheelchair." Miss McLeod herded us into the house, through the immaculate living room with its original wide-plank floors and stone fireplace. Karen's room was just what I wanted my daughter to have: crisp and pretty, with birds singing in the trees outside the window and a view of the countryside and the swimming pool.

There was no way I could feel unhappy about the school or apprehensive about leaving Karen there.

Before we left, Miss McLeod took us into the library. "You go home now," she said, "and don't worry about your little girl. She's going to be fine. Be peaceful about her."

I didn't really know who these people were or what they were going to do for Karen. I was just happy that they would keep her and that we could afford the school.

"It would be advisable," Miss McLeod said, "if you were not to see Karen for six months. Let us have her for six months, and you will be pleased, I think, by her progress. It will do all of you good to be separated for a while."

I said goodbye to my helpless daughter, sitting alone in her wheelchair, surrounded by odd people chattering to each other in German and French. I had never been separated from her. In my mind her whole existence depended on me, and in a few moments I would be leaving her behind.

When we reached home exhausted that night, I cried when I looked at her crib and the empty bureau drawers and the place in the closet where her dresses used to hang.

"She'll be all right, honey. It's a nice place, nice people." Richard was right. There wasn't anything lacking in the school.

"I won't worry," I promised him. "But I miss her. It seems so quiet and empty without her."

I did miss her. Now that she was finally gone, my heart ached for all the noise and confusion and upset that meant that Karen was in the house. At the same time, I had a sense of freedom for the first time in years. I could get up in the morning and send my husband and son off and go to work myself without the burden of Karen on my mind. It made my life, my marriage, seem bearable. It eased the tension between us, and because I was happier and more relaxed, I tried harder to make my husband happier.

We called the school every week.

"Karen is fine," we were told. "She's getting on well."

"Of course she hasn't forgotten you," Miss McLeod told me in answer to my anxious question. "Karen is a bright little girl."

It was the first time anybody had told me that.

The summer slipped by, a happy summer for us, then the fall. In early November Miss McLeod called us.

"We will be having a week's vacation at Thanksgiving. It's time for you to bring Karen home to be with you for the holiday. We'll be bringing the children to New York on the Sunday before Thanksgiving."

She told us where and when to meet Karen. Now we had two weeks of anticipation and uncertainty to get through before we saw her.

Chapter 10

THE BUS FROM THE SCHOOL was late reaching the meeting point where the parents of children from New York were waiting.

I was filled with an anticipation equal only to that of the day when I knew I could finally bring Karen home from the hospital. She'd been gone nearly six months. Regardless of the assurances I had had from the school, I didn't really know if she would remember me.

My husband paced around in the cold outside the car, smoking. We had left David behind with his grandmother, since we didn't know what to expect. Thanksgiving was a few days away. How thankful was I going to be?

The bus arrived, and parents crowded around their children who got off the bus unaided. Then someone from the school put Karen in her wheelchair and brought her over to us. She looked well and happy. She was laughing, and yes, she was excited to see us.

Was she the same child I had left at the school in June? I secretly imagined that her homecoming would mean a return, if only for a week, to the disruptions and demanding care I had been unable to cope with. I didn't believe anyone could help her, certainly not in such a short time. So it was with mixed feelings that I greeted my child.

"Here's your Karen," said a young woman from the school. "Doesn't she look pretty?" Karen reached out to me to be hugged and kissed and then made some sort of sign to the woman who nodded vigorously.

"We've made some progress with her sign language and Karen can express a few things. She just told me you were her mother. You won't have any trouble picking it up. Miss McLeod sent along a list."

Richard picked up the suitcase and put it in the car. I wondered if he had taken in what we heard: *Karen could communicate.*

"Did you leave us a supply of diapers for the ride home?" I asked the woman.

"Oh, Karen doesn't use diapers any more, Mrs. Brown. She knows how to tell you when she has to use the bathroom. She raises her hand."

"But . . . that's impossible."

"No, it's true."

It was true. Under her skirt she was wearing only a pair of cotton panties. If this was true, it meant we were free of an unpleasant part of caring for Karen.

"Miss McLeod asked me to remind you of one or two things," the woman was saying. "We only use the wheelchair when we take her long distances outdoors. While she's at home, she shouldn't be allowed to become dependent on it."

"What about braces?"

"We found they were too heavy for her. And they make her too different from the other children who don't have physical handicaps."

I was finding it difficult to take all this in. The next news astounded me.

"Of course," said the woman, "now that she's walking around—"

"She can't walk!" I said.

"Oh, not very well yet. She walks, holding onto a wall. Where there aren't any walls, she crawls. The important thing to remember is that when she falls, as she often does, she should be made to get up alone. She can't go through life expecting people to stop everything to pick her up."

The young woman started to walk back to the bus. Turning back, she called cheerfully: "I think you'll find her manners are quite good now."

We drove home, asking each other if we were dreaming.

"It can't all be true," I kept saying. Yet Karen sat beside me quietly for the hour-long drive. She wanted me to hug her and hold her, but there were no tears, no restless fidgeting.

We carried her in the house and put her down at one end of the living room. Richard and I sat on the sofa at the opposite end.

"Come to us, Karen." I held out my arms to her.

She watched us seriously.

"She can't do it," Richard said nervously. "She doesn't understand. Let me get her."

"Wait. They told us she could walk. Let her try."

Slowly, with the help of a chair, Karen pulled herself to

her feet. Then unsteadily, holding herself up against the wall, my baby took the first steps I had ever seen her take. She went only a few feet before she stumbled and fell. Instantly her father was off the sofa, catching her, carrying her to me. The three of us laughed and cried, treasuring one of our happiest moments.

All at once the house was filled with family and friends who had watched Karen grow up helpless. They had all come to see and celebrate this miracle in our lives.

Thanksgiving that year was one when I truly gave thanks. We had someone like a whole person living with us. Karen sat at the dinner table with her hands folded, waiting to be fed. (Because of her physical difficulties, she had made only slow progress in mastering the finger and hand movements necessary to hold a spoon; but she was learning.) She was quiet. She was eager to tell us all that she had learned. She was interested in everything around her.

"How did you do it, Miss McLeod?" I asked when we took her back to school. "How could you transform that wild child who couldn't or wouldn't communicate with us into a human being?"

"First of all," she told me, "we treat her as if there is nothing wrong with her. To us she is exactly like the other children who have none of her handicaps. She has no special privileges."

"We could never reach her. She couldn't hear us. She used to drive us crazy."

"We never give in to her. We try to push her on the way to being independent, but we don't allow her to deviate from our routine. She needed discipline and we gave it to her. We taught her to understand when she is being punished for misbehaving."

I had never known how to punish her, or how to teach her anything.

Miss McLeod said: "As soon as she behaved badly at the dinner table, we took her to her room and told her she was naughty."

"But she couldn't understand that—being naughty."

"She didn't understand the first time or the second. But no matter what she did, no one laughed or encouraged her. She was just removed from the room by one of the staff."

If Karen came crawling back and behaved badly again, someone else would take her back to her room. She was allowed to rejoin the group only if she sat quietly with her hands folded. The calmness and firmness of the school staff finally opened up her mind. She learned what other people expected of her, and when her whole attention was drawn away from herself, she began to learn other things as well.

The individual attention the children received from the staff, from persons not emotionally involved with them, as parents must be, yet who were dedicated to their work, made it possible for Karen's life to be turned around. It was a situation that could never have existed in her home environment, where my confused emotions about her, about David and my husband, about my work and my life, made me incapable of dealing firmly—and sanely—with her. It was, in many ways, the perfect situation for Karen, one that I had hit upon only by chance.

The method followed by Karen's school had been developed in Europe in the early part of the century by the Austrian philosopher, Rudolf Steiner, whose beliefs formed the basis of anthroposophy, which he called a "spiritual science." His schools for physically and mentally handicapped children, the delinquent and emotionally disturbed, are still maintained in various European countries by present-day followers of his beliefs. A couple who were anthroposophists themselves had started the school in Pennsylvania

(75)

not long before we took Karen there. With a staff of volunteers, mostly Europeans and followers of anthroposophy, they had developed their program and obviously, in the case of Karen, had met with considerable success.

Anything that Karen is now had its basis in the years she spent at the school. Besides the manners we saw on her first visit home and her ability to walk—which improved greatly over the years—she developed, with their help, her personal sign language with which she could convey a range of ideas, wants, needs, and emotions. She learned to count. She learned to read perhaps three hundred words. She learned simple housekeeping skills, as well as dressing and undressing herself. Her progress in a few short years was heartening. She wasn't the girl with a slight limp I had been promised, but neither was she the hopeless child who would never recognize me.

One weekend I went alone to Pennsylvania to see her. She had been at the school about two years then, and to my eyes she was still a miracle I couldn't quite believe. I found her in the kitchen of the farmhouse, on her hands and knees, patiently scrubbing the floor.

"What are you doing?"

"This is my job," she said in sign language. "I wash the floors."

She got to her feet to hug me, then looked back at the bucket of soapy water and half the floor left to wash.

"You sit here," she told me.

I sat and watched her scrub slowly and methodically, absolutely delighted with herself, proud to be showing me what she could do. Each child had household tasks to perform, and it was decided that Karen's job was to wash the kitchen floor each Saturday because that fit in well with her physical abilities.

The developing sense of purpose in her life during her

early years at school and her joy in accomplishing simple tasks couldn't help but make everyone around her joyful. I didn't stop then to consider what her future almost certainly would be. Instead I used to say to myself: this is real, Karen's life, being content with her little pleasures, the people she loves, having friends, making presents for me and the family.

"This is for you, this is your name," Karen said, pointing to a crude piece of sculpture with the word "Mother" on it.

Karen was well and happy. She seemed settled at last. I was at rest for two or three years, working to pay for her school and keeping my home going. We visited her as often as we could, short weekend visits when I saw her improving by tiny steps that were to my eyes gigantic strides, visits that ended in tears for her and me, because she clung to me and because I had to leave her behind.

As the years have gone by I have gradually come to realize that in those days I was incapable of admitting to myself that I was really the mother of a handicapped child. While her teachers and therapists struggled to develop her limited capabilities, I saw her moving along the road to normalcy. Somehow, someday, my dream daughter would emerge. The knowledge that I was now and forever parent to this imperfect child was too defeating for me to accept.

Was my husband happy? I didn't know. Our common joy at Karen's improvement didn't revive any of the love with which we had started our life together. We were more than distant; we lived out our lives with increasing hostility and tension. Perhaps he understood better than I the hopelessness of Karen's condition.

It needed only a crisis to show how weak the bonds were that held together my marriage, my life for ten years. It took a crisis to force me to take a genuine step toward personal growth, even though at the time it seemed less a step toward a new maturity than it did a plunge backward into despair and deeper guilt. Nevertheless, it set me in a direction I might never have taken; it pushed me into a journey of a dozen years of learning about myself and the world.

Chapter 11

༜

WHEN KAREN WAS TEN, my mother died and I left my husband. In this crisis I found myself, at thirty, starting all over again. The management of my life was in my own hands.

My mother, I discovered after she was gone, had been a silent partner in my life. She had devoted herself to me and the children, enjoying Karen's small triumphs and sharing some of the burden of her with me. She even learned to like her son-in-law. While she was well aware that all was not right with my marriage, she never interfered or even commented. Before my marriage she had questioned my undying love for the man I chose to marry at nineteen; later she was silent. But she was there.

It was as a grandmother that my mother found happiness after my father's death. To David, she must have been the only genuine bright spot in his life. His mother worked, his father wasn't a demonstrative man, and both parents had an antagonism for each other that must have been obvious to a bright nine-year-old. His sister had been taken away from him when he was seven. But his grandma was always there to bring him presents and spoil him, to take him on outings, to give him boundless love. In her way, my mother was extremely important to us.

When she told me that she was having minor surgery, it was just another in a series of operations that stretched back fifteen years to our Philadelphia days.

"Yes," her doctor told me, "it's a minor operation but potentially dangerous. Your mother's weight"—she had gained and gained until she weighed nearly 250 pounds—"presents a tremendous hazard."

I brooded about it. It was more than just another small operation. I knew she should have special nurses after surgery, but she certainly didn't have the money for them, and neither did we. I become obsessed by the idea that my husband should be intuitive enough to know that this was something I wanted desperately to do for my mother.

I was helped along in my self-pity by the fact that on the December weekend preceding Mother's surgery on Monday morning, we were scheduled to have Richard's cousins to our house. As I shopped for the party, I thought how ludicrous it was that I was spending money to entertain a group of people who meant nothing to me, and yet I had nothing to give my mother.

I had my party on Saturday night and visited my mother

on Sunday for what turned out to be our last conversation.

"What did you wear? How did the table look?" She was interested in every detail.

"I wore that blue dress, the one you like. The table was beautiful. I found yellow chrysanthemums."

"And they liked the food?"

"The food was fine."

We frittered away the afternoon in idle talk about the party, the cousins, who did and said what.

"Larry and I will be here tomorrow after the operation. I'll be at work all day if you need me." Mother was in the hospital where I worked in the public relations department.

"I'm going to be fine, Helene. Tell your brother not to leave work for me."

Monday seemed endless. The operation took seven hours, and it was only late that night that the doctor told us as reassuringly as he could that Mother was resting comfortably, that my brother and I could end our vigil and go home.

By 11:00 P.M. I had called my aunt and a few relatives to give them the report and was about to fall into an exhausted sleep when the phone rang.

"Get dressed quickly," my brother's voice said. "We have to get back to the hospital. Mother's dying."

A nurse would not have saved her, dying as she did from complications of overweight and years of poor health, but my guilt over her death exploded. If I had been a better, more caring, daughter, she might not have gotten to this stage. She was only fifty-two. There was no reason for her to die. It was my fault—and my husband's.

I flung myself into an orgy of fury and self-pity: It was my husband's fault that my mother had died. He didn't help me. He had never helped me. He was selfish for wanting to give that party, for depriving me and my mother of our final comfort. He had always hated my mother, and now he was glad she was dead. All this, in addition to a real and deep grief over the loss of the one person in my life who had been a constant.

It has taken me a good many years to see through myself, to take some of the blame I placed on my husband. Only time and self-knowledge have taught me that the world is not seeking to soothe and satisfy me, that I—that no one— can expect to have something given that isn't asked for. People, even a husband of eleven years, are not mind readers. It is a very immature belief: thinking the world is waiting to give you exactly what you want without the asking. Now I can set my priorities and see my goals realistically, but at thirty, still a child in all but years, all I knew was that things weren't turning out as well as they were supposed to.

I spent a week in mourning for my mother, brimming with bitterness and grief. My only thought was how and when I could leave my husband and how I would survive. I was convinced, without understanding the implications of such a move, that I would survive better than I was surviving now. Maybe in June, I thought, when David is away at camp. The shock won't be as great for him. Then again, I thought, maybe sooner, as I looked at the man who was sharing my home but no other part of me, who didn't know how to comfort me even if I allowed him to.

I didn't allow him to. My tears, my grief, were mine alone. I shut myself off in the bedroom, my face pressed into the pillow of a unmade bed. I dressed only for callers paying their condolences in the evening. Grief-stricken, David roamed the apartment. The woman who had been the anchor in his life was gone, and his parents lived in a state of barely disguised warfare.

Then, a week after my mother's death, Karen came home from school for the Christmas holidays.

"Where's my grandma?" she asked immediately. Grandma was always there to greet her at the beginning of a vacation. She would hug and kiss Karen. Grandma loved her. There was a present in Karen's suitcase for her.

"She's gone," I told Karen in sign language, the tears running down my cheeks.

Karen knew at once that something bad had happened. Her grandma was gone, and her mother was crying.

I told her slowly and carefully in sign language: "Grandma got sick and went to sleep. She is gone. Forget about her."

Karen started to protest. Nothing like this had ever happened to her.

"Forget about her," I said emphatically.

"Grandma?"

"Yes."

Karen looked at me for a long moment and then burst into tears. She pulled herself up on the wall and stumbled around the apartment until she came to the picture of my mother on a bookcase shelf. She carried the photograph over to me, thinking perhaps she had misunderstood me.

"This person," she said, pointing to the picture, "this person got sick and went to sleep and forget about her?"

"Yes."

Karen took the picture to a bureau, opened the bottom drawer, and put the picture inside, face down. She didn't mention her grandma again for a long, long time.

By the end of December that year, I had decided that I wanted all my grief over at once. I wanted an end to the marriage. Now. I still might have weakened, postponed the inevitable until June, for another six months, another year, except for the New Year's Eve party.

On New Year's Eve our next-door neighbors gave an

informal party for friends in the apartment complex where we lived. "Bring the children," they said. "All the kids are going to be there. We won't be up much past midnight."

I could hardly rouse myself from my depression to get my hair done and put on party clothes. I didn't want to leave the apartment and mingle socially, even with friends who had been with me during the weeks of my grief. But I was persuaded and I went.

Richard carried Karen to the next apartment and sat her down. David tagged along and then went off with his friends to watch TV and play games in the next room. People were nice to me. Someone always seemed to be next to me, talking about children and apartments and this and that. I began to feel civilized for the first time since Mother had died.

Out of the corner of my eye I saw my husband head for the bar. He seldom drank anything, but this time I saw him down a couple of drinks in rapid succession and retreat to an armchair with a third in his hand. He was never comfortable in large groups, but tonight he withdrew completely and watched the party with a sullen expression. I didn't pay him much attention.

At midnight someone started singing "Auld Lang Syne," the kids crowded in from the other room, husbands and wives kissed, friends embraced. I looked across the room at the man I was planning to divorce one day. We didn't kiss or touch. We didn't say, "Let's forget about the bad year just passed; let's start over."

Our hostess bustled in with food for the buffet. Wives started filling plates for their husbands, and people began sitting down in groups, talking quietly and eating. Playing the role of dutiful wife before our friends, I went over to Richard.

"Can I get you something to eat? Is there something I can do for you?"

He looked up at me from the chair, the years of heartache written all over his face for everyone but me to see. I was too blinded by my own grief to see his pain. I only saw the man I wanted out of my life.

Slowly he stood up, not drunk, but made brave, perhaps, by a few drinks. He looked down at me and spoke loudly and distinctly, stopping every conversation around us. "The only thing you can do for me is drop dead."

The room was utterly silent as he walked out. It was as if he had smacked me in the face in front of our son, who watched wide-eyed and scared from a corner, in front of our friends and neighbors before whom we had always performed our happy-couple act.

I kept back my tears long enough to somehow get the children home and into bed. Karen was irritable from staying up late, and David couldn't understand what had happened, only that it wasn't good. Then I shut myself in the bedroom. *I don't deserve to be humiliated like that. If I'm not much of a wife to him, he's not much of a husband.*

I spent the night raging against him. In the morning, when I emerged from the bedroom to find him asleep on the couch, I asked him to leave, leave now, for good. He answered with silence. Maybe he didn't believe that I meant it, that I could manage alone, that I had the courage to be on my own.

He finally agreed, reluctantly, to move out. He left me and our children believing that I would want him back. I was to him the little dependent nineteen-year-old he had married; I wouldn't be able to survive without him. He tried to prove it by paying my rent and for Karen's school while I worked to support David and myself.

"I don't want to get back together with you," I told him. "I want a divorce."

He wouldn't answer me. I had no money; I had no idea how to get a divorce; but I knew the break was final. He waited for me to come back to him, but I knew I never would.

The year that followed was one of the worst in my life. I couldn't shake the grief and guilt over my mother's death. And I was alone. For the first time in my life, I was all alone, a thirty-year-old woman who had gone from her mother's house to her husband's without ever being an independent person. I had to feel my way slowly in a world where I had only a partial personal identity. To a certain group of people, I was an interior decorator. Otherwise, I was a woman who used to have a husband, who used to have a devoted mother, who had no friends except those from my married life who had known me really as only half a couple. My little girl was away. I had David, but it seemed impossible to explain to a nine-year-old who had just suffered the loss of his grandmother why his father had now disappeared from his everyday life. It seemed impossible to tell him why his future would be better if he didn't have to live with parents who had grown to hate each other.

Through all my confused emotions, one thing was clear. I felt that the weight of the world was gone from me, that my decision to get a divorce had been the right one. There was no more trying to please a person I knew I could never please.

Richard knew it was too late, that we would never put back together our broken dream, but it took until he decided to marry again, years later, for him to agree to a divorce. He sent David to camp in the summer. He took David to stay with him on weekends. He drove to Pennsylvania to see Karen. He visited her when she was home. After the first sharp bitterness had subsided, ours was a "friendly separation."

With my husband gone, I had a lot to think about. It was one thing to be disappointed with my marriage and the life I had. It was another to be solely responsible for whatever kind of existence I wanted.

Chapter 12

࿏

A NEW LIFE. Freedom. Caring for myself, my children, taking on responsibilities. New experiences, a constant struggle to find out who I was, a constant search for an elusive happiness I knew must be there somewhere for me. No longer sure exactly what "perfect happiness" consisted of, but again certain that I would recognize it when it happened to me.

Fourteen-year-old Helene, in her flowered and flounced bedroom in Philadelphia, her daddy's darling and the perfect little girl, never dreamed she would end up the way she did. Her life didn't turn out like a story in the pages of a woman's magazine. Instead I spent tearful weekends with a retarded daughter, painted my nails in the latest shade, and went every day to an office in Manhattan, wearing a fur coat I paid for by myself over months and years. I cried my eyes out night after night because nothing was the way it was supposed to be. And realizing, at long last, that I didn't have the faintest idea how things *were* supposed to be, I decided that if I was going to survive, I had better find out fast. I set out to become someone I could be proud of—if not as a wife-mother-homemaker, at least in the work I was doing.

The road to success for women in business in the early sixties was, in retrospect, something of a comedy routine. So many talented, able women endured the mild humiliations of job-hunting in a society blind to most skills except the ability to tame an electric typewriter.

Do you take shorthand?

No.

Can you operate a switchboard?

I didn't know how to do that either.

Dictaphone? Addressograph? Mimeograph?

No, no, no.

But I could type.

I still hoped I could find work in the decorating field, but I was not so hopeful that I forgot about the weekly paycheck. I couldn't bring myself to remain at work at the hospital after my mother died, so I made the rounds of agencies, looking for temporary office work that would allow me to keep up my decorating a day or two a week. The agencies didn't find my potential very impressive.

"We see that you're separated and have a school-age child," they said, looking over my sparse résumé. "What if your son got sick? We have to have people we can rely on."

There were simply no jobs for me. I quickly learned to

lie, as thousands of other women had to lie—to deny in the job market their almost shameful state of marriage and motherhood.

"I'm single. I have no dependents." It seemed that everyone could read this shocking lie on my face. And if they didn't notice the lie, then they were surely pitying me for being a poor thirtyish spinster with no home and no children and no immediately salable abilities.

"Yes, I can take shorthand. Of course I can run a switchboard."

What I wanted to say was: I'm an experienced professional decorator. Find me a job in that field. Mention of my decorating background only produced slight smiles. I couldn't be that good if I was looking for a temporary job.

What I ended up with was a series of jobs for a week here, three days there, two weeks someplace else, where I spent a lot of time trying to hide my lack of office skills from my temporary employers.

The struggle to keep life going took all my time and energy. I went to the offices where I was sent by the agency and tried not to think too hard about what my life lacked in the way of friends and social life and close relationships. But as Karen settled in more and more at her school, and her life and mine went separate ways (except for my periodic and traumatic visits to her) and David became more involved with school and friends and growing up, my loneliness became unbearable.

People said: "You're a good-looking woman. You must run into a lot of men in those offices where you work. You'll find yourself a boyfriend before long."

They were wrong. I didn't meet a lot of men in those offices—married, single, or divorced. Executives don't flirt with the temporary typist whose desk is placed at random somewhere out in the hall. And even if I had struck someone's fancy, I would have been thoroughly at a loss. I simply had no experience with casual male-female relationships. Nothing in my background had prepared me for going out and meeting men with a light touch. But romance was another matter. It was serious. It ended in marriage.

"Miss Brown," said the woman at the agency, "we have an interesting five-day-a-week job starting next month in June. However, it's permanent, and if you take it, you'll have to stay. It has something to do with houses and decorating."

I said: "It sounds like just what I'm looking for."

Jack Nelson was sitting in an almost empty, two-room office suite on West Fifty-seventh Street when I arrived for the interview. He must have been near sixty, and to me that was old.

"I want a girl Friday," he said. "Think you can do that?"

By this time I had learned to say yes to questions like that.

"Married? Got any kids?"

"Well . . ." The impulse to tell somebody something about me came over me. He seemed like a nice, older man. "As a matter of fact, I was married, but I'm separated. I have an ten-year-old son."

"You don't look old enough."

"I have a daughter, too—a year older. She's handicapped, at a special school in Pennsylvania."

"Say, that's too bad. Is she doing OK?"

"She's doing wonderfully. You wouldn't believe how much she's improved since she's been there." I poured out the story of Karen and my life. He was the first person I'd encountered who accepted her matter-of-factly. I loved Jack for that; he made me feel relaxed for the first time in eleven years.

"I suppose you have to work pretty hard, with all those

responsibilities," he said. "Now this'll be a one-man office. Not really hard work. I'm doing the promotion and publicity for this group of home-builders. They have these three houses and the furnishings, and they want to franchise them to other builders around the country."

He got out some promotional material to show me.

"I coordinate all this stuff and get a percentage. Think you'd like to work for me? We'll have a good time."

"All right," I said. "I'll take the job."

"Fine. You come in Monday. I'm getting in some office furniture over the weekend. We'll order supplies on Monday and get to work. I've been in the publicity business a good many years. I'll show you my scrapbooks next week when we have some free time."

I arrived Monday, prepared to do whatever a girl Friday did.

"Now—Miss Brown? Mrs. Brown? Helen, is it? Ah, Helene. This'll be your desk. You make a list of the things you'll need. No, first you go out and get some coffee and Danish, and I'll show you my scrapbooks. Give you an idea of the things I've done."

At least I was going to have someone to talk to. It was going to be different from sitting in solitary splendor at a leftover desk in a hallway.

"Here are my scrapbooks." Jack put a pile of them on my desk. They went back to the twenties and were filled with photos and releases and news stories.

"I was a copper king way back then—and a millionaire."

Sure enough, there was a picture of Jack as a young man, together with a beautifully dressed woman. The caption read, "Copper King Jack Nelson with his wife, former Ziegfeld Follies star. . . ."

"Of course, I lost my money, so I stopped being a copper king. I got into publicity. Worked with a lot of big stars."

There they were, smiling out from the scrapbooks. "Married quite a few times. I'm married to a real nice woman now. She works, and I've made a few good investments, so I'm OK, but I took this job so I'd have something to do. How about getting us some more coffee? There are a couple more scrapbooks I want you to see. Then we'll get down to work."

It didn't take me long to figure out that whatever it was Jack and I were supposed to do, it wasn't much. He was as glad as I was to have someone to talk to. I bought a lot of rubber bands and paperclips and pencils and envelopes that we never used. I even went in on Saturdays with David and got paid overtime. But I did very little work.

Yet to me, it was glamorous. I'd never known anyone who had been a copper king, friend to movie stars, married to a Follies showgirl, and a warm, good-hearted friend, all in one.

"Helene," Jack said one day, "you ought to find yourself a man. No point in a young woman like you spending all your time alone."

I started to protest that at thirty-one, I was hardly a young woman, especially considering my nearly grown-up children.

"Nonsense. When you're my age, you'll realize how young thirty-one is."

"Anyhow," I said, "I haven't thought much about it." But I had. "I don't have the time."

"Plenty of time for romance, if you want to make the time."

The truth was, I was more like someone seventeen than thirty-one. I'd hardly been out on a date in my life. There had been no grown-up-get-dressed-and-do-the-town dates.

"Put yourself in the right frame of mind," Jack advised. "You're too young to be at home with your kids for the rest of your life."

One Saturday when I didn't have David with me, I was walking from Jack's office to the subway when a handsome man stopped me to ask directions. I knew somehow that he really wanted to talk to me.

Well, Jack, I thought, let's see if the right frame of mind is all it takes.

"Where are you going?" the man asked after I had told him how to get to the New York Public Library or some such place.

"To the subway. Home."

"Can I walk with you?"

"Well, yes, I guess so."

"I'm just in town for a few days, from Florida." He gave me his business card. "Can I take you out someplace tonight?"

"Yes," I said. I wasn't in my right mind. I didn't know this man.

I met him at his hotel. I was driving a borrowed car, so I could come into the city and meet a stranger for a date and go home by myself.

"Let's have a drink here at the hotel," he said, "then we'll go out to dinner."

"Fine," I said. (I came from a family who never had a bottle of liquor in the house.) "I'll have a whisky sour."

I was out with a handsome, suntanned man from Florida, having a drink at an expensive hotel bar, going out to dinner, and then dancing. Dancing? I'd never gone out dancing in my whole married life.

I never saw him again. We said good night and I drove home to Long Island, feeling like Cinderella in her ballgown. Maybe Jack was right after all.

In contrast to the life my big "date" represented, my real life was pretty bleak. I talked on the phone constantly to my married friends who lived around me. They thought my life was glamorous because they were stuck at home all day with their kids. I thought they had everything.

I still had that romantic dream of a Prince Charming coming along, exactly the same dream I had had as a teenager. But I didn't know what to do about it. I had no single friends who could guide me in the so-called singles world that was just starting to be popular. I had an idea that there was a world out there that I should know about, where a single woman wasn't invisible, unfortunate, or a joke. But not knowing how to approach that world, I did nothing except cry at night from loneliness and show up at Jack's office every morning.

Toward the middle of summer, Jack said: "Sweetie, I've got some bad news for you. My people have decided they're not going to keep this office going. I'm OK. I don't have to work if I don't want to. But I'm worried about you."

"I'll be all right. I can go back to temporary jobs and decorating."

"Not enough security for you and your kids. Their father isn't going to sit still for the rest of his life. He's going to find somebody to marry sooner or later, and then he's not going to give you one cent more than he has to."

I didn't want to think about that possibility. Richard was devoted to his children.

"Listen to me, sweetie. You get yourself a real good job, one with a future, and some nice fellow of your own."

I listened, but I didn't believe him.

"I guess I can't convince you," Jack said. "But I'm not going to close up this office until I find something for you. You're a crackerjack secretary. You'll have no trouble getting a hundred and fifty a week."

I knew perfectly well that I would indeed have trouble getting a hundred a week from anybody who was a real businessman.

(95)

"Don't worry. I know a lot of people. I'll try to line up something for you."

The next day, he had some news.

"I called a friend who works for a big magazine publishing company." He reeled off a list of major magazines, including one, a home-decorating magazine, that was my bible. All the years I was a decorator, I used to sit and read every word of it each month. I would look at the masthead and think: Those lucky people who do this kind of work. What lives they have. They must be so intelligent, so sophisticated. I saw them sitting in glorious offices. They were beautifully dressed and groomed. They went out to marvelous lunches with celebrities. They traveled. They wrote columns and features about magnificent homes and designs. They were gods and goddesses. I was awestruck that such people existed.

"I told my friend that you were a super executive secretary," Jack was saying, "and if there were any openings, they'd better grab you."

Oh sure. I knew I wasn't suited to be anyone's executive secretary. I was good at buying paperclips and getting coffee and Danish and talking to Jack.

"There's only one job open now," he said a few days later. "One of the magazines has a new editor-in-chief who's starting in October. She needs a secretary. Are you interested? It's that decorating magazine."

I was speechless.

Jack had a little grin on his face. "I thought you might be interested. As a favor, my friend will arrange an interview for you with the new editor."

I thought to myself: There's no way I'm going to get that job. But Jack believes in me. I can't tell him no. To Jack I said: "Have your friend make the appointment. And thank you."

Chapter 13

ॐ

"THIS IS WHERE I'm going to get found out." A more nervous person had never appeared for an interview. Someone would surely figure out that I was a highly recommended secretary who couldn't take shorthand, an executive secretary who didn't know what an executive secretary did.

But I dressed very carefully for the interview: black dress and white coat, with white gloves and little pearl earrings. I was hoping to look like whatever it was I should be.

"Please sit down," said the blond, blue-eyed receptionist. "Mrs. Thomas will see you shortly."

Mrs. Thomas had been named editor-in-chief of the magazine not long before. Before that, she was a vice-president of a major department store. She was taking over at the magazine in a couple of months.

A young man came in, slim, blue-eyed, darkhaired, cleancut. I was beginning to get a funny feeling. Everyone so far looked *exactly* the way they should. I touched my elegant little gold pin for security.

"Miss Brown?" He looked down his perfectly straight nose at me with absolute disdain.

"Yes."

"I see that you come well recommended." He glanced at a letter in his hand.

I was afraid to look at him.

"Do you take shorthand?"

"Yes, sir." I sat demurely, hands in their white gloves folded, my legs crossed at the ankles, wondering who I was talking to.

"You type, of course?"

"Of course."

"How fast?"

"Sixty words a minute." How did I know how fast? I never had to type sixty words a *page* for Jack. But sixty words a minute sounded good.

"I see that you are an experienced executive secretary . . . office manager . . . ordered supplies . . ."

Jack had done a good job of promoting me.

"If you'll just wait"—he was trying to be very important— "Mrs. Thomas will be free to see you in a few minutes." He disappeared into an inner office.

I was completely cowed by his superior manner and expensive pinstripe suit. My only comfort was in thinking that he probably couldn't type well or take shorthand either.

Suddenly a Presence appeared.

A tall person walked into the office. Her gray hair was in an elegant bun, and she wore a black silk dress, with a fox boa slung around her neck. An entourage followed her, taking notes, listening to the orders she issued as she swept in.

I felt as if I were watching a stage play.

My friend in the pinstripes guided her over to me and introduced us.

"Hello, my dear. Come along." She swept me into her office. "Miss Brown, is it? I'm so happy to meet you. Now sit down here. I'm going to need you so much. Can you start on the first of October? That will be my first official day here. That's the day you and I start hard at work together."

I was dazzled. I was overcome by her. I said I could start October first.

"Wonderful," she said. "We'll have a wonderful time. I'd love to talk more, but I have some French visitors waiting to have lunch with me."

Mrs. Thomas gathered up her papers and her fur boa. "Do you have a family, my dear?"

"My son is nearly eleven. I'm divorced."

"A son. Isn't that marvelous? I have a twelve-year-old son. Won't that be fun? We both have boys almost the same age."

At no time did she talk about the job—what I was supposed to do, whether I could do anything at all, or about salary. I didn't care.

"Oh, my dear, I just know this is going to be so wonderful. I'm looking forward to working with you. You're going to be such a help to me. I'm so nervous about coming here." She looked intently at me. "It's such a relief to know I'll have you here with me."

If she was nervous, I was a wreck. But Mrs. Thomas had the capacity to make you feel that she just couldn't get along without you.

(99)

"I'm so happy." Her eyes misted up, and then she was gone.

Apparently I had a job as executive secretary to the editor-in-chief without lifting a finger, without opening my mouth, without taking so much as a typing test. I had been promised a good salary, just as Jack said. Nothing had ever been so easy. And even as I sat across from that elegant woman behind that impressive desk, I was saying to myself: Someday I want to be sitting behind a desk like that.

"Thank you, Jack. I got the job."

"I knew you would, sweetie. Anybody'd be crazy not to hire you. I sure will miss having you to talk to, though."

"I'll miss you, too, Jack."

"Be sure to let me know how that little girl comes along. And don't forget what I told you about finding a man. You need a nice guy to take you places, show you a good time."

"I'll remember."

"Well—" He looked around the office. "All this will be gone in a couple of days. I suppose it wouldn't hurt to close up early today. I'll take you to lunch to celebrate your new job."

I had more than a month before I started work at the magazine. Thanks to Jack and his overtime pay, I had a couple of hundred dollars extra, so I decided to take a vacation, something I hadn't done since my parents used to take us to Atlantic City each summer. I wasn't ready to become a swinging single, but I also wasn't ready either to close myself up completely in my apartment until the end of my days.

When a married couple, friends from my own married days, mentioned a resort they'd been to the previous summer, an "intellectual" resort with daily guest speakers on the arts and literature, it sounded interesting. And it was inexpensive. I didn't know how to bridge the gap between being married and being single or the secret of what single women did, but at least I could improve myself intellectually.

"It's very nice," my friends told me. "In New Hampshire, on a lake. It's a beautiful place, and not full of single women looking for men. A lot of couples go for the intellectual stimulation, but you'll meet some single people too."

David and Karen were both at camp. I was all alone. I didn't even have Jack and his office to go to.

"All right," I said. "If I'm going to start a whole new life in the business world, maybe it's time to start with a new personal life too."

The resort brochure seemed to promise just what I was looking for—all those intellectual activities, as well as swimming and tennis and golf and evening get-togethers and dances. Never mind that athletic activities weren't my strong point, that I wasn't especially good at easy small talk, that the so-called literary world I read about was completely alien to me. I sent in the money and packed my borrowed luggage.

I had never been on an airplane. I was scared to death. It was only when I was in the limousine that took us from the airport to the resort in New Hampshire that I opened my eyes and paid attention to the people I was with: girl after girl after girl. Nineteen years old, twenty, twenty-one; false eyelashes, fancy hairdos, makeup, cleavage. And me. No couples, no intellectual types.

I don't think this is going to be so good, I thought.

I had only been in my room a few minutes when a hearty gym-instructor sort of girl of twenty bounded in with her suitcase and tennis racquet.

"Hi," she said. "I'm Janet. Which bed is mine?"

I had a roommate. Before I could answer her, the door

opened and another twenty-year-old marched in with a set of matched luggage that held, as it turned out, an astonishing array of beautiful resort clothes.

I had two roommates. I could feel the numbers of my age slowly being spelled out on my forehead: "31–31–31. This woman is thirty-one years old. Her children are ten and eleven." I felt like a dowager trapped in a nursery school, and worse, I was only another single, just like them.

Dinner was agony. I tried to make conversation with the college senior on my right and the recent secretarial school graduate on my left. Both were decked out in halter tops and long skirts. I passed the salt in my modest, high-necked, long-sleeved, ladies' luncheon dress. The males at each table for eight averaged one pale timid man for seven exuberant young women.

I was sitting alone at the after-dinner dance, watching all those glorious young women dividing up the few available men between them, when a voice said: "You look so unhappy."

I looked up and saw an extraordinarily handsome, blond college boy. I'd never seen anyone like that, even when I was in high school and seriously looking for them.

"Hi, I'm Paul. I'm the water-ski instructor." He flashed a dazzling smile at me. "I saw you weren't dancing, so I thought I'd come over to cheer you up."

I pulled myself up haughtily, dowager and mother once again. "This was a mistake for me. I'm obviously out of place." And I poured out my life story—how old I was, how old my son was (I didn't feel like getting into Karen with this young stranger), that I was newly separated, that I didn't know any single people, that my well-meaning friends had sent me to the resort, and that I was probably leaving in the morning.

"Don't go home tomorrow," he said. "There are new people coming every day. You'll find somebody interesting to be with." He turned his dazzling smile on me again. "I've been working here every summer since I was in college, except when I was in the army or living in Europe."

Paul wasn't quite the child I had imagined him to be. He was twenty-six, in his last year at law school. I thought he was one of the nicest people I had ever met. We talked and he went off and danced with some of the other wallflowers. Clearly part of his job was keeping women like me from leaving in despair at the sight of all those healthy young bosoms and the meager supply of young men. It seemed to work; I felt better.

The next day Paul was more dazzling than ever, in white tennis clothes, standing beside me when I rose from the breakfast table.

Some mother must be proud of that boy, I said to myself, still caught up in my devoted-mother role. Some girl is going to be very lucky.

"So you're not leaving after all," he said. "Come take a ride in the motorboat before I have to give a water-skiing lesson."

I'd never been in a speedboat, either, but I had managed the plane, so I should be able to handle this. He took me around the lake. After lunch he walked me around the golf course. In the evening I was looking around for him to rescue me from an amorous man who suggested ending the day's fun in his room or mine (and mine already had a gym instructor and a Jewish princess, even if his advances hadn't terrified me). Paul rescued me, and in two days we were the best of friends. I was having a wonderful time.

On the third night, after I had nervously downed two martinis at the weekly free cocktail party (clear gin looked harmless in comparison to the pinkish Manhattans on the tray), Paul took me out on the dance floor and something happened. Before the evening was over, I was embarked on a summer romance with a college boy, a lovely, hand-holding, heart-throbbing romance. We were inseparable during the rest of my stay there. We walked around the golf course hand in hand, danced close at night, and kissed passionately at the door to my room. My innocence was such that it didn't occur to me that romances went further than that if you weren't planning to get married. The last time I'd felt that way I *had* gotten married.

"I'll drop you a card," he said at the end of the week when the limousine arrived to take departing guests to the airport. I looked back to see him waving and felt a pang at the end of the romance, at waking up from a short dream of what Prince Charming should be.

"Just wanted to let you know," went the postcard that arrived three days later, "that someone was still thinking about you after you left."

"I'll be back in the city next Friday," said the letter two weeks later. "I'll call you that night. Get two of the best tickets for *The Fantasticks* for Saturday night. You'll love it."

If there was anything I wanted and needed, it was a man who knew what I would love.

"You look great," he said on Saturday night. "We'll have dinner in the Village before the theatre. Where's your son?"

"He's with his father for the weekend."

"I can't wait to meet him. Let's go."

Before we left I noticed that he'd left the money for the tickets on the kitchen counter. I loved him for that.

I loved the whole evening—the dinner, the theatre, everything. I loved stopping for a drink after the show and holding hands in a dim bar, being close to him. So different from the long years of my marriage when there was no excitement —mental, physical, or sexual. By the time he brought me home there was no question of a kiss at the door. I was totally infatuated with this wonderful person in whom I chose to see no faults. I was delighted by his introduction to the world of New York restaurants, classical music, theatregoing, spur-of-the-moment fun, dancing the night away. Candlelight dinners at my apartment, love-making. It was all so different, not only from my marriage but from any part of my previous life.

I treated our relationship with care. I felt I was so incredibly lucky to have found Paul that I shouldn't do anything to disturb it. Thus Karen remained carefully hidden from him. At any moment he might decide that I was too old for him after all (the five years' difference between us loomed very large on nights when I lay alone in my bed with my ten-year-old son asleep in the next room). Paul might decide that I wasn't worthy of his attention, that the role of a twenty-year-old adoring girl friend didn't fit me, that, above all, the mother of a mentally and physically impaired child was not a suitable companion for a young man at the threshold of his adult life.

Chapter 14

ᑌ

Aᴼ FEW HECTIC WEEKS in September with Paul marked a small but significant turning point in my life: I had managed to pick up the thread of my youth and begin to grow in terms of men and women, of myself and the world. To be sure, I was blind, almost willfully blind, to the problems that accompanied my newfound relationship, but this is hindsight. At the time I was terribly happy.

An even more significant turning point occurred on October first. It was my destiny to be beginning my new job in an antiquated building on Madison Avenue. Not mine and Karen's, not mine and my husband's, but mine as an independent person going to do a professional job. Karen was part of it, the child whose existence had forced me out of the house into a different world. Richard was part of it. He had helped to open the door of our suburban apartment by refusing to recognize what I needed at home. But what I did, I did by myself, because of my conviction (not too well thought out, but absolutely certain) that life was not meant to be a sellout to circumstances that are difficult or situations that seem impossible.

My first meeting with Mrs. Thomas had been so hair-raising that I had scarcely noticed the place where I was going to be working—the palace of my editorial gods. I examined it now.

Gray and hospital-green walls, mismatched desks and chairs, bookcases with books and papers spilling out of them, cracked linoleum floors. It looked, in fact, like a lot of publishing offices I came to know, but at the time I realized with a shock that there was nothing "beautiful" about these shabby surroundings.

The first day I discovered a ladies' room with a bare bulb hanging from the ceiling and rust stains in the sink where the water dripped continually.

"I'm Helene Brown." I introduced myself to a middle-aged lady sharing the broken mirror.

"Oh, Mrs. Thomas's new secretary. Welcome to the magazine." She introduced herself.

She was my second shock. She was the woman who had been my idol for years, who had written wonderful columns and articles for the magazine about finding just the right embroidered organdy curtains for a newlywed's first home, just the right piece of furniture for a star's Manhattan apartment, just the right color tile for the kitchen of an executive's new house in Darien. For years I had read her stories, marveling at the perfect taste she displayed, believing that a sleek, glamorous woman had gone out and found all those curtains and tiles and had come back to the office to tell the world about it. Wrong. She was in her fifties, wearing plain clothes, a motherly looking woman whose hat as often as not was crooked and who had a magic talent for turning out superb copy. She was my first experience in this world where, I had supposed, the people were more sophisticated than I was, more elegant and tasteful. No one was what I had imagined them to be. They were really just like me, a little insecure, ignorant of certain things, sometimes petty, sometimes brilliant, but basically ordinary people.

Mrs. Thomas, on the other hand, was another story. She was bigger than life and as glamorous in her way as anyone I had ever imagined. I idolized her. I was born to serve her.

I got to the office early every morning to put fresh flowers on her desk and wind the clock. I made appointments. I ushered in and out of her office the most famous names in the decorating and fashion and cosmetics world. I took charge of her expense account and cashed her checks for her and got her gloves cleaned. I answered her telephone. So high was my station that it didn't matter that I wasn't a great typist. I had a secretary to do that.

My pinstriped friend, Bob, passed in and out of the office. We circled each other warily, competing for Mrs. Thomas's attention. It took a while before I stopped feeling intimidated by him. It was two years before we became the close friends we are today.

It was a mindless job, I suppose, but I was important to Mrs. Thomas. And I desperately needed to be important to someone. It wasn't a conscious goal—learning the magazine business—but that happened too. After I had been there six months I knew how things worked, what people did, about studios and advertising and how stories got written. Gradually, without being aware of its happening, I knew that I could do anything I wanted to in this business.

All of it made up in some part for the lingering pain of Karen who was never far from my thoughts. (After all, I didn't really deserved my good fortune, did I, having sent my child away from her home?) I had Paul, too, who made up for a lot. (Did I deserve him either? As it turned out, I didn't, or at least some frightened, guilty part of me decided I didn't.)

Some new confidence in myself in terms of my work and my ability prompted me to approach my boss on a level other than social secretary.

"Mrs. Thomas, I'm not really a secretary."

"Nonsense, my dear. You're a perfect secretary."

"I mean, I'm really *not* a secretary. I'm a decorator."

"How very nice. That means you really appreciate all this we're doing here."

She didn't believe me, and it didn't make much difference to her anyhow, as long as her needs were taken care of.

"Mrs. Thomas, I want to do something at the magazine that has to do with decorating."

"But you are, my dear. Of course you are. You help me so much. I don't know what I'd do without you. I certainly wouldn't want to lose you. But I do want to do something for you. You just be patient, and I'll see what I can do."

"I hope you'll remember—"

"As soon as I can, I'll make you my executive assistant, and we'll put your name on the masthead right next to mine. Won't that be exciting?"

It sounded exciting, and the promise kept me at my desk. Fortunately, I was able to continue my own decorating practice as jobs came along.

Our offices were right in the center of my decorator world, at Fifty-sixth Street and Madison Avenue. When Mrs. Thomas took her two-and-a-half-hour business lunches, I got my decorating work done. When she sent me to the milliner's to pick up a hat, while they were wrapping it up I ran into a fabric house to get some swatches. On the way to a jeweler's to have her rings cleaned or a necklace restrung, I dropped into a floor coverings showroom to argue about an order. Picking up airline tickets, I managed to look at new furniture.

I was patient for nearly two and a half years.

"Mrs. Thomas," I finally said, "I've heard a rumor that there are plans to add a new person to the decorating department. I hope when there's an opening, you'll give me a chance. You remember I told you how much I wanted to do something in decorating."

"We'll see, my dear. It depends on what the decorating editor wants."

I went to the decorating editor, a sweet, older, Southern woman.

"I've spoken to Mrs. Thomas about working in your department. I've been a decorator for almost ten years, and I can show you pictures of what I've done."

"Honey, I can't just take you away from Mrs. Thomas. Why, we all know how much she depends on you. But I'll speak to her if you like."

To me, Mrs. Thomas said: "My dear, I know you should have the job in the decorating department. You'd be perfect for it. I want you to have it. But I need you. I don't know what I'd do without you."

I thought: You'd find another Helene Brown overnight if necessary. Aloud I said: "I hope you can find a way for me to go to the decorating department."

Finally she gave in. I was made an assistant decorating editor with a raise of eight dollars a week. All I had to do was find my replacement.

I was busy training her—the world being full of young women eager to work at a magazine doing anything at all—

when I heard from a friend about a job that was open at another major decorating magazine.

"It's really the kind of job you should have," she told me.

After all the effort I had put into getting my new job, I wasn't especially interested in one at another magazine.

"But the decorating editor is looking for an associate design editor. She wants someone who's a decorator, who knows how to do rooms and sets."

It was a better job than the one I was getting.

"I think you should call her," my friend said. "What have you got to lose?"

I really didn't have anything to lose. I was interviewed and hired.

"Mrs. Thomas," I said a couple of days later, "I don't know how to tell you this, but I'm leaving to take a job at another magazine. I'll be doubling my salary. I have to do it."

Mrs. Thomas rose to the occasion. She'd already lost me anyhow, and her new executive secretary appeared to be as keen as I had been about serving her.

"Oh, my dear. I'm so happy for you. What a wonderful opportunity. You're going to be such a success. But I don't know what we'll do without you." She cried real tears and smothered me in her bosom.

Then I cleaned out my desk and began four years of hard work as associate editor in the decorating department. I was an editor at last. I had a title and was doing the work I knew how to do best. I didn't know at the time how much I still had to learn, but I had a new sense of security and a feeling of being authentic and important in a job for the first time in my life.

The rest—the part that involved Karen, the part that related to my social and personal life—wasn't so serene, however. Only when I was completely wrapped up in my work did Karen fade into the background, and perhaps for that reason, my work became extremely important to me. Still, she was the secret part of my life—my excuse, real or imagined, when happiness eluded me. The cord between us was stretched thin by distance, but if Karen fell, my life also fell. And if I fell, Karen would have no life at all.

Chapter 15

K AREN BROKE UP my romance with Paul. I believed this
for years. By the time I left Mrs. Thomas behind, and the
fetching and carrying, I also left behind my glorious romance.
I had been seeing Paul for a couple of months when I began
to wonder how serious our relationship was getting. The
teenager in me still saw all love affairs ending in marriage. I
behaved and felt more like a young woman his age than
mine, because I was doing a lot of catching up on the time
I had missed by marrying young and blindly. I was having a
carefree romance, so I steadfastly suppressed the disquieting
thoughts that crept to the surface when we weren't out
dancing and dining and having a good time.

Is this right? I'd ask myself in the wakeful nights when I was alone. He knows about David, but he doesn't know a thing about Karen. It's as if she didn't exist. If we were ever to marry . . . I didn't know how to face the problem, how to break the news about Karen and make it come out all right, how to keep Paul and the excitement and romance he brought me and at the same time admit the reality of my situation to myself as much as to him.

At first it was easy to avoid the subject. There wasn't much personal conversation between us. We kept things passionate and impersonal, a perpetual summer romance that didn't fade with the tan. I knew little about him, and he volunteered nothing. He had parents and a younger sister somewhere in Connecticut.

I argued with myself: I don't know how Paul will feel. If he loves me, as he says he does, he'll love Karen. She's a beautiful child. She doesn't look handicapped. But to someone who didn't know her, who didn't see her beauty through the eyes of a loving mother, she was obviously handicapped. It is my shame and my guilt about my child that is keeping me from bringing Karen and Paul together. Why am I so worried? She won't ever be a financial responsibility to him if we should get married. I can handle that with my salary and her father's contribution. I knew, though, that Karen would be an emotional responsibility for any man I married.

Paul is going to be rich and successful. He's aggressive and bright and charming. He'll be a wonderful lawyer, and he can deal with anything. He thinks I'm strong and capable. That's what he cares about in me. Karen made me that way, the necessity of coping with her. He'll welcome her and love her.

I worked out scenarios stretching far into the future, but never once did I think how Paul's life would really be affected: a young man with his whole life ahead of him, married to an older woman with two children. All I cared about was how much I would lose if he didn't like Karen. She's away at school most of the year, I said to myself. She'll always be away. She's made so much progress. How could anyone not love her?

I kept asking myself questions, but never the right one: why was I so insecure about myself that I laid the entire burden of my future on Karen?

Christmas time. Richard and David and I went to Pennsylvania to bring her home for the holidays. Paul was to be away until the last week of Karen's stay. I would tell him then.

We brought her home to my apartment in Manhattan. I was renewed, as always, by having her with me, and she was overjoyed at being home with David and me. It wasn't like visiting her at school. Each time I drove up to the door of the school, whether it was alone or with her father, I was unprepared for the psychological shock.

I was never prepared for the moment of parting, either, when Karen got down on her knees and held my legs, locking her arms around me, sobbing and sobbing, begging me not to leave. She was pulled away from me, and I looked back from the car to see a stricken little face that haunted me all the way back to Manhattan and for days afterward.

Holidays were different. To Karen, three weeks were forever. She had everyone she loved around her. We did things together. We ate out at restaurants and sometimes went to movies. Her father came to the apartment to see her each evening after work.

It was a fine, snowless December that year. I planned to take Karen for a walk down Madison Avenue to look at the Christmas windows. She wasn't able to stay on her feet continuously for more than a short period, although she was now able to move freely around the apartment unaided. I rented a wheelchair for our excursion.

Karen didn't want any part of it. She glared at it and me. She no longer used a wheelchair at all.

"Mother's going to take you outside for a walk," I said. I put my hands to my temple like blinders, the sign for looking, which she understood. "We'll look in the windows. I'll push you in that chair."

Karen shook her head violently and spoke to me urgently in sign language. "No. Forget about the wheelchair. I walk." She tried to push the chair away to show how much she disliked the idea.

"No, Karen. You walk in the house. Outdoors you have the wheelchair."

Reluctantly she allowed herself to be put in the chair. I was thinking of Paul. How could anyone not be inspired and delighted by my little girl's independent spirit and her desire to be like other people?

We waited for a light to change at the corner of Eightieth Street and Madison Avenue. A whitehaired old lady bundled up in blankets and in a wheelchair was pushed up alongside us by a nurse. Karen looked at her curiously for a moment, then she turned to me and gave me a dirty look.

She pointed to the old lady's wheelchair. "See that chair? Forget about it. See that lady like my grandma? That's not me." She shook her head emphatically and started to get out of the wheelchair.

"That's not me." It had occurred to Karen that her infirmity and the old woman's were different. She could walk. She could get out of her wheelchair if she wanted to. She wasn't an old lady.

We walked. People stared at the little girl awkwardly making her way down Madison Avenue beside a woman pushing an empty wheelchair. But Karen paid no attention to the stares; she was thrilled to be out walking on the streets of New York, looking at the decorated store windows. She had her mother with her. Maybe that made it all the more exciting for her, to be able to look at the empty wheelchair and know that she didn't need it.

Paul must see this, I thought. He'll love her. He'll be proud of her, just the way I am. I have to tell him now, before she goes back to school so he can meet her. Perhaps one day we would all be a family together.

I was a coward. I postponed calling Paul until the last day of Karen's stay, and then it was too late. I would do it in the spring instead, when Karen was home for another vacation. I gave myself three months' grace, three more months of untroubled happiness.

The week before spring vacation, Paul took me out dancing. He was graduating soon and had already lined up a job as a law clerk in a prestigious New York law firm. He and the two classmates he shared an apartment with were splitting up to find their own apartments.

"I saw a great four-room apartment today," he told me as we danced. "It's not a new building, but it has a lot of character. You could sure do a lot with it. The kitchen is terrific—you'd turn out some great pot roasts there."

I began to wonder what he was getting at.

"It's not a full two-bedroom apartment, but there's a small room off the foyer that could be made into David's bedroom."

I didn't know whether to hope this was a proposal or not. I'm not sure Paul knew what he meant, but I did know that the time had come, finally and unavoidably, to tell him about Karen. If he was that close to asking me to marry him—and I was willing to accept—there was no way I could escape this time.

Karen arrived, excited to be home, with a bag full of gifts. I sent her and David to their father's apartment for the day and sat Paul down to talk to him.

"I have something to tell you that I should have told you

about before, long ago." Suddenly I was in a panic. It was hard to get the words out. Paul just looked at me.

"I suppose I should have said something right at the beginning, but you'll understand when you hear."

He looked nervous, which certainly wasn't helping me.

"You know, people sometimes don't tell everything about their lives and what's happened to them, even to someone they love."

Paul nodded. Why didn't he say something? He was suppose to be in love with me, wasn't he? Hadn't we been seeing each other for nine months? Hadn't he been on the verge of proposing to me only a couple of nights before? We should be able to say anything to each other. The thought flashed through my mind that by hiding Karen from him, I had betrayed his trust in me. It was a bad way to start a marriage, if that's what the future held.

"It's not so bad, Paul. It's just that I have a daughter, too, not just David. She's a year older. She's handicapped. She lives at a school in Pennsylvania." The words tumbled out as I tried to make up for the months she had been my secret. "You'll love her, Paul. She doesn't interfere in my life. I want you to meet her and know her."

Paul looked as if he wanted to run out of the room.

"She's home now. She's staying with her father. I'll tell you the whole story."

I did tell him the whole story, with many tears. I relived the bad early years and the recent ones of improvement and hope. Paul was quiet and withdrawn, but he seemed to be taking it well.

"Let me bring her to meet you. Please, I know you'll like her."

He agreed to wait until I brought Karen home. I thought she looked beautiful, so healthy and happy.

Karen always liked men, and she decided she liked Paul. She immediately wanted him to hold her on his lap.

"You're not my daddy," she said to him in sign language. "You don't sleep here. This is my mother's house."

I told him what she had said, trying to make it sound light, the amusing comment of a child, the private joke between adults.

"No," he said seriously, "I'm not your daddy."

I could see that he wasn't at ease with her, although he was trying to be affectionate. As I watched them, a tight knot of anxiety in my chest, Karen's handicaps were suddenly glaringly apparent: her crippled hands and fingers that didn't move easily; the tilt of her head that wasn't quite right; her kneecaps flattened from years of crawling; the sounds she uttered, squeals and shouts that she couldn't hear; her ungainly walk that I was so proud of.

"I have to get back to the apartment, Helene. I promised the fellows I'd help them move some of their stuff. Goodbye, Karen."

She didn't want him to leave. I didn't want him to leave, with everything somehow unresolved.

"I'll call you tomorrow," he said. But he didn't. He called a week later, and we went out for a dinner filled with tension and uneasy conversation. Karen wasn't mentioned. I didn't see Paul again for a long time.

Karen had driven Paul away, and it was the end of my world. She'd had a lot to do with breaking up my marriage, and now she had broken up what might have been a marriage. In the midst of my soul-searching I never paused to consider that I myself wasn't ready to marry a boy who was starting out as a law clerk, earning $7,500 a year. He wasn't ready to take on any kind of responsibility and certainly not one like Karen. I'd forgotten that when we were out together and there was a younger woman around, I was always in a panic, thinking he was surely going to want her more than me. At the years went by, I could only feel this more strongly. It didn't occur to me that even before he knew about Karen, he hadn't pursued his half-proposal. He'd caught himself before he committed himself to a marriage and a life that would be filled with complications even without her. Meeting her had only confirmed what he had already decided not to do.

But that's not what I saw at the time. I blamed myself and Karen as one. I had made a mistake by not telling him earlier. I had made a mistake by being her mother at all. Because of her, I wasn't worthy of a good man.

Forget men, I told myself. Nobody's going to snap me up and take care of me for the rest of my life. I'll take care of myself and my kids just the way I've been doing all along. Nobody wants to get involved with a woman who has a handicapped child. I'm not going to let my heart be broken again.

It was a fine resolution, but with Paul gone, I was back where I began, as far as loneliness went. We hadn't had a wide circle of friends, and I certainly had few of my own. I'd grown pretty far away from my married suburban acquaintances and had never been close to people who shared my interests; there had been no time, no opportunity.

David had a mother who came home and cried or who was so busy working at the office that she didn't get home until late—and then cried. He was at the age when boys go through all the rotten phases boys go through, when he wasn't doing well at school and was hostile at home. I knew I had a responsibility to give him as much of my time as I could, but I was so wrapped up in my troubles that I often substituted feeling guilty about him for time and attention.

When I needed a friend most, Margaret showed up at the

magazine one day. She was a new addition to the staff, a writer, and I thought she was a bit odd—short clipped hair, plain clothes and glasses, pleasant but quiet. Not my kind of person, I concluded, having almost no experience in knowing what kind of person mine was.

"I'm having a little party at my place," she said. "I've asked a couple of people from the office, and I thought you might like to come."

I was about to refuse automatically, but then I said: "Yes, I'd like to come." I couldn't bear another evening at home alone.

"I have a place in the Village," Margaret said. She gave me the address. "It's informal, just neighbors in the building, a few people I've met since I came to New York."

"Where are you from?" She'd recently come to New York and already she had enough friends for a party? I'd lived there fourteen years and couldn't have rounded up enough people to fill up the chairs in my apartment.

"Chicago. This is my first job, and I'm finding it so interesting."

I looked at her. She was at least twenty-seven, and certainly didn't look like a rich girl who had never worked or a divorcee starting out all over again.

Noticing my puzzled expression, she laughed. "Oh, I was in a convent for a number of years. I left it last year and came to New York. People are coming around eight."

Margaret had a walk-up apartment that she shared with another young woman. It was filled with people the likes of which I had not encountered before, people from different places and different backgrounds, making their way in New York City.

"This is Ted." A bohemian artist, I thought. "This is Janet, my roommate." A woman in her twenties, from Ohio. "This is Claudette, who lives across the hall." From Trinidad, exotic and beautiful and remote. This is so-and-so. A jazz musician. Another jazz musician. Artists, writers, photographers, secretaries, starving actresses, young men from ad agencies.

It was the kind of life that was totally unfamiliar to me. I'd never lived with a roommate, never had girl friends who lived across the hall, men friends who dropped in casually, oddballs and earnest nine-to-fivers, everyone following different paths, free and unencumbered, enjoying life. It gave me a new perspective. You didn't have to be somebody's wife, somebody's girl friend. You didn't have to get tied up in knots about relationships and secrets.

Margaret and I became fast friends: an ex-nun from Chicago and a Jewish girl from Philadelphia.

When Margaret returned from a weekend at the Newport Jazz Festival one summer, she was transformed. She had sat beside a young Englishman at the festival, and they'd talked jazz, Margaret's passion, the whole weekend. They had fallen in love, just like that. A twenty-eight-year-old woman who'd been out of the convent scarcely a year, and within six months of meeting him, she was married.

"You and Claudette take care of each other," she said at the wedding. Then she was gone to live in England.

If it's so easy for her, I wondered, what's wrong with me? I knew what was wrong: me and my handicapped child. Me and the defect of my life that was never going to go away. Margaret had everything going for her. I didn't. I wasn't a winner, and nobody picks a loser.

Fortunately, I still had my work. I had landed a huge, private decorating job for a new house that was being built on Long Island. It was a wonderful opportunity for me as a decorator, and I was going to make the most of it.

Never mind men. Love and marriage were for people like Margaret who deserved it.

Chapter 16

ॐ

ALAN CAME WITH the decorating job on Long Island. He was an architect, a soft-spoken, gentle man with a special quality about him that was almost mystical. He held strong beliefs about architecture and had a look of tragedy in his eyes. It was the tragic look that attracted me.

Before he even said anything, it was clear to me that he too had experienced pain. And when he did speak, everything he said sounded terribly profound. Working together and talking about our mutual client, Alan and I built up a deep rapport. He was the male friend I needed. I wanted friends badly, now that Margaret was gone and her friendly bohemian circle had disbanded. True, I had sort of inherited

Claudette from Margaret, not realizing how genuine and lasting the friendship between us would become. Claudette and I were close, and our long phone conversations about life and love, about this and that, were important to me; but Alan seemed to supply something that had been missing from my life.

Did I fantasize, then, about a deeper relationship with Alan than our strictly business one? That vulnerability that attracted me, the idea that I could take away the tragic quality that hovered around him—these were all mixed up in my hope that I would still find Prince Charming once and for all, before it was too late.

For me, it turned out to be too late. Alan asked me to dinner, and I phoned Claudette for advice. "This isn't going to get serious, I know," I said, hoping it would. "He's so businesslike. But is this supposed to be a date? Do I go home and change my clothes or do I appear casually at the restaurant as if I were coming straight from work?"

"You're a grown-up woman Helene. You should be able to tell if it's a date or just business."

"I can't tell. Lunch during a working day is business. But this . . . He's just not the kind of man you know that about."

"Oh, great. Another man you don't know about." (She'd heard a lot about my life by now.) "Go home and change. From what you say, he doesn't sound as if he pays all that much attention to whether you're dressed for a date or not. You might as well be dressed for it. Where are you going?"

I named an expensive French restaurant.

"In that case," Claudette said, "it's probably a date."

I put on a black dress and met him at the restaurant. It wasn't business, but it didn't seem exactly like a date either. We talked about our work, then he started to talk about himself. He was divorced. He had left behind three children in another state with his ex-wife. He'd come to New York to make a new career for himself, but the loss of his children troubled him deeply. He loved them so much, and he suffered because he couldn't be with them to enjoy them and watch them grow up.

He was someone just waiting to be picked up and made well.

I talked about David and my life, but not Karen. There was no point in bringing her into a conversation between two business acquaintances. It's just another pleasant evening, I told myself.

It was until whatever magic it is that happens to two people started happening. It was no different than when I was sixteen or when I saw Richard walk through that office or when I went out onto the dance floor with Paul. We talked until they closed the restaurant. As we left, he took my hand —and that was it. We fell into a taxi and into each other's arms.

My romance with Paul had been an experience that grew out of my being starved for physical affection. In Alan, I believed I had found the man I had been looking for, the perfect combination of father, lover, brother, confidant, and friend. Alan had great strength and inner resources. He would be able to take care of me. And I would take care of him. I would make up for what he had suffered in the loss of his children.

We quickly settled into a routine in which we were virtually inseparable. Breakfast together and dinner, endless telephone conversations in between, talking about his work, my work, our lives. His humor sparked mine and we laughed together about everything, something comparatively unknown to me. I lived for the weekends when David went to his father and we could spend every minute together.

I felt completely a part of Alan. Except for Karen. Each

time I started to speak of her, I remembered Paul. I remembered how telling him about her had seemed to spell the end of our relationship. I couldn't do that to myself again. Then I remembered how not telling him had been equally destructive. Yet when Alan spoke to me of his children, his eyes filled up with tears. In the end it seemed better to tell and get it over with.

"Darling," he said after I had cried out the story, "of course I love her already, just because she's part of you. And I'll love her more for herself when I know her. When can we go to see her?"

When Alan met her he scooped Karen up in his arms and smothered her with kisses. She immediately became our child, not just mine. My happiness was complete. A happy ending was on the way at last. We would be married someday.

Alan and I embarked separately on hectic work schedules. I began at my new job, and he went to Atlanta on an assignment that kept him away for several months. The separation was unbearable, but each day brought a letter more loving than the day before. I felt I knew him completely, his thoughts and feelings. Although we had been together only a short time, I was convinced that there were no hidden corners, no part of him that I didn't understand. It was an illusion, of course, but a happy one. I knew myself so little that it was impossible for me to understand anyone else.

I worked a punishing schedule, knowing that my future depended on my success, that Karen's future depended on mine, whether or not Alan and I got married.

The decorating editor for whom I worked was a professional, no-nonsense lady who knew how to get the most from her associates. She was a good teacher for me: I learned by going out and doing what had to be done. I was constantly challenged to do things I was sure I could never do. But I did them, and each success gave me such self-confidence that I went on to the next task enthusiastically.

I started arriving at the office at eight-thirty, only to find that my editor had been there since eight. I stayed each night until six-thirty and later if there was a copy deadline or if a photo session lasted late into the evening. David suffered the most. The decorating editor asked me when she hired me, knowing I was separated and had a child at home, how I would manage.

"I have a housekeeper," I lied. "I can handle the job."

Many was the time that David stayed home alone with a temperature while I went to work.

"This job requires a good deal of travel. You will have assignments in many parts of the country and will have to leave on a few hours' notice," she had told me. I assured her there would be no problem.

When she would call me into her office in the afternoon and tell me I was going to Texas or Massachusetts or some-place else, I would rush home to pack up David and send him to stay with his father.

I put my job first, because I knew that long after David was grown and gone from my house, my work might still have to support his sister, who was never going to be able to care for herself.

In spite of the hardships, I loved my work. I couldn't wait for Alan to get back for good so I could have the man I loved with me, as well.

Alan was back. He was loving and concerned. He was interested in everything I had to say about my work. It was wonderful.

But something was wrong. From time to time his temper flared for apparently no reason. He began to complain that the people at his office were meddling unnecessarily in his projects. He protested that he hated social functions connected with business; but he attended them eagerly. He resented the time I spent away from him and began to accuse me of having a secret life apart from him. Then a minute later, he would be holding me in his arms or we would be chatting amiably about David's schoolwork, or we were laughing until we cried about some silly occurrence.

I was uneasy. When we did quarrel, the battle raged violently—in person, on the telephone. One night when I met Claudette for a drink at a midtown hotel, I caught sight of Alan darting around a corner as we left. He was spying on me. It frightened me that he had followed me and even more that he didn't trust me. Increasingly his gentle, loving moments turned into long, angry, irrational harangues.

"I think you're sick," I finally told him. "Mentally ill. I don't know how to deal with you any more. And I'm getting to be as sick as you are."

My love for him was as deep as ever, even deeper because I felt he needed me so. Yet slowly, insidiously, I was being infected by his sickness. The pattern of violent quarrels and subsequent tearful making up was becoming ingrained in my life. It was a vicious, destructive way of life, and I began to relish lashing out at him when he attacked me with some unreasonable statement.

Reluctantly, he recognized that he wasn't well and agreed to see a psychiatrist. The marriage we both believed was in the near future was postponed until he got into his treatment. When he felt like a "whole and healthy man," we could plan our life together.

Chapter 17

I BREATHED A SIGH OF RELIEF when Alan started seeing Dr. Wolff, because I had been presented with a new dilemma.

Karen was now fifteen. The annual end-of-school festival was a week away. David and I were going, as was Karen's father, who always accompanied us to major school functions. I got a call from the school.

"When you and Mr. Brown are here for the closing of school, we'd like to have a talk with you," was all the director said, a new woman whom I didn't know very well.

I tried not to imagine what it meant. I knew Karen was reaching a difficult time in her life. I knew the school had been changing over the years, growing larger and more impersonal as it became better known for its successful treatment of the handicapped. Karen's progress depended on working daily with someone on a one-to-one basis. When the school was small and a staff member could spend half an hour a day just with her, she was stimulated and interested in learning. Without that attention, she was bored and directionless.

"Mr. Brown and I expect to arrive about midday," I told her.

"We'll plan to see you after the pageant, then, in the administration building." By now the school had built several new houses; instead of the comfortable, homey farmhouse, there were residence houses, offices, and workshops.

With my worries and premonitions, I called Richard.

"We don't *know* that the school wants her to leave," he said. "You're imagining things. Wait till we talk to them before you get upset."

The comfort of knowing that she was safely settled in the school was important to me; I'd grown accustomed to it. When her life was taken care of, I was able to deal with mine. I tormented myself some more, anticipating the coming interview. If they didn't want to keep her any longer, I would be faced with keeping her myself or finding another place. In the first instance, it would mean radically altering my entire life-style, which I didn't want to do. No matter how much Alan loved Karen (and he did), I simply couldn't cope with both of them. My work was important to me, too, not just because I liked what I was doing, but because I had to have it to support us. It was clear that Alan was in no position, or condition, to marry me. Even if he were, my husband and I had still not yet been able to agree on a divorce, and it would be a long time before I was free to remarry. As for finding another place, I was more aware than ever of how hard it was to find a school for a child like Karen.

Then, convinced that they were sending her away, that they would hand me a little crippled, deaf girl with her suitcases packed, I began to wonder why. Perhaps it was because I didn't visit her every other week, the way some of the other parents did. I knew that when I didn't see her for long periods, she began to disrupt the routine of the school, begging for her mother to come.

"Is my mommy coming? I want my mommy." She would sit by herself and cry, refusing to do anything.

Still, it was bad for both of us to see each other too frequently.

Maybe they didn't want to keep her because she was too different from the other children. When I visited there, I was conscious of the fact that I wasn't like the other mothers. I was a New York businesswoman whose stock in trade was an ability to compete in looks and dress in the world where I worked. I wasn't a suburban housewife any longer, just as Karen, with her luxurious hair and pearly teeth and bright eyes, was not a typical handicapped child. We were both oddities among exceptional children and their parents.

Maybe Alan's paranoia had infected me.

Another wretchedly hot June day—outdoors in the baking sun, indoors for refreshments—with Karen pulling at me, demanding to be fed, to be listened to, to be taken home.

Marion McLeod had retired as head of the school and was devoting herself entirely to physical therapy. I didn't have the rapport with the new head of the school that I had had with her, and I felt (or imagined) a certain antagonism from the director toward Karen and me.

When Richard and I went to her office after the festivities, all my worst fears came true. She said: "We regret that we cannot have Karen back in the fall. As far as we are concerned, our work with Karen is over. Our mission is to help as many children as possible. When a child reaches a point where we can no longer help her, it is our obligation to free that space for another child who will benefit from our programs."

Even expecting this news, I was crushed by it. "What are we going to do then?" I was intimidated by this stern, businesslike woman and could barely get the words out.

"It is extremely difficult to place a child like Karen, but surely a state institution in New York would take her. Other than that, we have no recommendations."

"What about your vocational training program?" I had counted on that. The school had a training program for children aged fifteen to eighteen, where the students learned a simple trade. At eighteen they moved on to a self-supporting village run by the school, where in small workshops they made bread, dolls, candles, and other things for sale. It paid for their keep, and they had a productive life at the same time.

"We do not feel that Karen would benefit from the vocational training program," the director continued. "All our programs are designed for hearing, ambulatory children who are able to participate fully in group situations. I'm sorry to say that Karen wouldn't fit in. She still requires too much help from others." She stood up. "I regret that we can be of no further help to Karen."

I wanted to beg, to say, *Please, you must help me; I don't know what to do.* But I sensed that it wouldn't do any good. All I could think of was that Karen was coming home—to my apartment—for two weeks, my two weeks' vacation that I took every year in June so I could get her ready to go away to a summer camp for the handicapped. And when fall came, she would be back in my apartment with no place to go.

Marion McLeod, frailer and even more spiritual, met us we were leaving the office.

"Mrs. Brown," she said, "I've learned that Karen is not coming back. I'm sorry to see her go. I'm so fond of her and so proud of her progress."

"I don't know what I'm going to do, Miss McLeod."

"Karen has very special needs. I know how difficult it is to find a suitable place, but—"

I didn't need buts. I needed help, real help. Then.

"But there's a school nearby that I've visited. It seems quite nice. I don't know much about the program, but I think Karen would be happy there until you found something more suitable. I'll give you the name of the woman in charge."

One door closed and another opened.

We brought Karen home. I sent her to camp and called the school Miss McLeod had mentioned.

Yes, the school had an opening. They understood the scope of her handicaps. They could take her in the fall. It wasn't an educational facility. They had no training programs. It was a custodial facility with various activities to occupy the children.

The tuition was twice what we had been paying at Downingtown. It was Karen's home for the next five years.

Karen's departure from the school where she had learned so much, and the anxiety I had until she was settled again, frightened me badly. I saw more clearly than I had for years—since I first mustered the courage to send her away the first time—what it would mean to me if someday she really had no place to go. The need to make a secure future for us began to nag me. If Alan wasn't ready to marry me yet, he might be soon. According to him, he was much better, and he insisted that the fears and problems that had been plaguing him were being worked out with Dr. Wolff's help.

But I still had a husband standing in the way of my remarrying.

I have another life, I decided. I'm never going back to Richard. The longer I go on, not rocking the boat and accepting his contributions to the children, the harder it's going to be. At the first opportunity, I intended to discuss the divorce with him. The chance came when he called one day and took me out to dinner. All through the meal, I could see that he was working up to something. Finally he said: "It's been four years. I don't have any kind of life."

Thank God, I thought. He finally wants to get things finished and over with.

"I don't think you have any kind of a life either, Helene."

"You're wrong." He had glimpses of my sometimes frantic business life. He knew I never had any money. But he didn't see—or chose not to see—that I had a full life in spite of the difficulties. "You're wrong, Richard. How many times do I have to tell you?"

"You're still struggling."

"But I've bettered myself. I have a job that's a stepping-stone to an important career. If I'm struggling, it's because I have a lot of financial obligations and my work is hard. But I don't see any of it as a bad thing."

"I don't see the sense to it. I think we ought to get back together."

I looked at him in disbelief. How many times *could* I tell this man who was apparently blind to the fact that I found my single life, however difficult, preferable to going back to living with him.

"You can't change my mind," I said. "I really think we ought to get a divorce. The sooner we're divorced, the sooner you'll make a life for yourself without me. You'll meet someone and want to get married again."

He refused to talk it. The problem was again deferred. I tried to discuss it with Alan.

"Are you sure you're not planning to go back to him?" Alan was continually suspicious of me. Just when I thought we were having a sensible discussion, the way we had at the beginning of our relationship, he'd turn irritable and belligerent. Apparently Dr. Wolff was not helping much in that area yet.

"Of course I'm not going back to him. I love you." His irritability aroused a lot of hostility in me.

"We'll talk about it later. I'm meeting someone in an hour. I don't have time to discuss it now." He mentioned a man in the publishing business whom we both knew.

"Why are you lying to me, Alan? I saw him the day before yesterday, and he was leaving that night for England for two weeks."

"What were you doing seeing him?"

"I just ran into him at lunch. What's the matter with you?"

"Nothing's the matter. Quit nagging me."

"I'm not nagging. I just want to know *why* you lie all the time. And they're stupid lies, things I can pick apart in a minute. You tell me you've been one place when I know perfectly well you were someplace else. I could name a hundred instances."

"Look, if you want to quarrel, go right ahead; but I'm leaving now, so you'll be talking to yourself."

Alan's compulsion to lie seemed terribly unhealthy. Tiny, inconsequential lies, meaningless and completely transparent. I sometimes wondered if Dr. Wolff knew about this, and if so, how he felt. It was damaging our relationship, that much was certain. To Alan, it was becoming a game for him to lie, and an equally sick game for me to take the lies apart and start a vicious quarrel. I was becoming a shrew, never trusting anything he said or did, constantly carping at him, always suspicious. He had turned me into his twin, so I was feeding on the need for the uncertainty, violence, and grief he caused me. I allowed it to go on and on.

I refused to listen to people like Claudette, who hinted that she could see that something bad was happening to me. To me, it was an example of how friends failed to support me.

The facade of my life was beginning to crumble, and I was scarcely aware of it.

Chapter 18

ℰ

My lingering insecurity about Karen was increased by the friction with Alan, by the unresolved situation with her father, and by my own apparent compulsion to punish myself with regard to all of them.

A day spent with Karen at her school was a repetition of the other torments I put myself through. The joyous part of the day was the moment I walked through the door and she saw me. Her face lit up and she came to me, tumbling over her feet in her haste, falling, laughing, putting her arms around my neck to snuggle close to me.

Then she looked up at me and asked, "Where is my daddy?"

"Your daddy is far away," I told her. "You will see him later."

"How many days?" She held up her fingers so I could count the days.

"More days than that. Forget about it."

We went out to lunch at a nearby restaurant on the highway. Karen never stopped asking questions. "When will I see my brother? Where is Uncle Alan? Where is my daddy?" Where, when, how long . . .

She knew that once we had reached the restaurant, there was nothing else we were going to do. We would eat, take a drive, and she would go back to the school, and I would go away.

"I don't want to go back to the school. I want to go home with you. Pack my suitcase. Take me home. How many days until I come home?"

It broke my heart to watch her run through her whole sign language vocabulary. I didn't know when she was coming home. I didn't know the answers to any of her questions. She tormented herself and me. Her thought processes weren't developed enough for her to appreciate the immediate moment, to allow her to separate the pleasure of seeing me from her longing for home, where vacations meant that she was constantly loved and hugged and indulged.

"I want my daddy, I want my brother, I want to go home." Like a broken record.

I wanted to scream at her: *Shut up, leave me alone,* as if she could hear me and do it. Instead we drove around the countryside in a rented car, half the time with her head in my lap sobbing, half the time with her pulling my hands from the wheel, trying to tell me something. We were two people going around and around, punishing ourselves, with nothing getting any better.

(138)

On desolate, wintry days I drove to Pennsylvania thinking, *If I have to make this trip one more time, I won't be able to face it. I can't ever do this again. The next time I have to go through this, I'll drive the car off the road.* There was a bridge over a river that we used to cross during our drives. *I'll just let go of the wheel, and Karen and I will go over the bridge into the river, and it will all be finished.*

Yet at the same time, Karen loved her school and her friends. She attached herself to the head of the school, turning her into a sort of mother figure. She insisted that the woman come to her room each night before bed so Karen could tell her the story of her whole day.

"What does she tell you?" I asked the headmistress. I was curious. My time with Karen, on vacations and visits to the school, was filled with intense and, for her, abnormal activity. I had little opportunity to see her in everyday circumstances.

"Oh, she tells me about all the important things that have happened to her during the day. She cries, she's happy, she reads. Maybe she will eat a lot or feel sick—whatever has stayed in her mind during the day. She's always very busy. She's friends with all the other girls."

True, when I brought her back to the school from a vacation in New York, the girls came flying from the house: "Karen's home, Karen's back."

"This is my mother," Karen always told them proudly. "I was home with my mother."

Then a look came over her face as she worked out a difficult mental problem: she didn't want me to know how glad she was to be back with her friends, but at the same time, being back meant giving me up until the next time. She didn't want me to know how committed she was to her school and the girls there.

The same thing would happen when I picked her up to

take her away to be with me in New York. She didn't want the headmistress, her special person, to know how happy she was to be leaving.

"I'm going home with my suitcase," she told the headmistress. "You come too."

"No, I'll stay here and I'll be right here when you come back."

Karen tried to persuade her. "No, come, come," pulling on her while holding my hand. A few obligatory tears to show how unhappy she was to leave.

Then, in the car she turned back in the direction of the school and threw kisses. "Goodbye, school." She pretended it was the end for her and the school.

"Forget about that place," she said to me. "I'm never going back. I'm not going to sleep at my school again. I'm going to sleep with you. Say yes." She nodded vigorously to make me say yes. Then she held up her fingers to make me tell her how long she would be with me—ten, twenty, hundreds of days. If she got past twenty, it meant to her that she was going to be with me forever.

"You know," I said, "you were just crying because you were leaving your school. Now you're saying that you're never coming back. Don't you love your teachers? Don't you love your school where you read and play and have friends?"

Karen looked at me. She didn't know what to say. I had caught her. She loved her school and she loved me. She loved me so much that whenever it came time for me to leave her, I couldn't even kiss her goodbye because she would start sobbing—no fake tears this time—and would have to be pulled away from me. I got into the car, as often as not, sobbing myself, to drive back along the Pennsylvania Turnpike, trying to regain my strength and serenity to face another week at work.

(140)

So many times I thought: *This is not working. It's an open wound that won't heal. Where is the end to this? Is it going to be my entire life?* When she was home, I sometimes thought: *Why doesn't she drown in the bathtub? It would be easy for her to slip. Why doesn't that happen?* Or I would be sitting in the kitchen and hear her in her bath, making a noise that sounded like an emergency. I would keep right on with what I was doing, not going to her, thinking: *I'll go in later and find that she's drowned.*

At that moment Karen would appear, drying herself and laughing, and I would be overcome with horror and guilt at my thoughts. How could I feel that way, loving her as much as anyone could love another human being?

At the same time I was locked in that mutual torment with Alan whom, I believed, I loved as much as I could love any man. And I was working long hours for a demanding boss, at a job to which I was totally committed.

In this way months and then years slipped by. I tried to see the improvement in Alan that he claimed was obvious to him. As I stood screaming at him over some trivial lie, I would wonder how nearly three years of psychiatric treatment had helped him. It certainly hadn't helped our relationship.

After one horrendous day of quarreling, I called Claudette and we drove to Long Island for dinner. With the help of a tranquilizer and Claudette's sensible conversation, I managed to calm down. I decided that this was the last time I could allow myself to go through a scene like that with Alan. It was Saturday, and David was with his father. I could go home after dinner and be alone and get some kind of grip on myself—and maybe my life.

Alan was sitting in the lobby of my apartment building, waiting for me. He looked so sick and sad that I didn't have the heart to turn him away. In my apartment we talked quietly, for a change, about our three years together and what was wrong with our lives.

"I know I'm still sick," he said," and I'm going to stick with my analysis until I'm cured. Darling, I need your help more than ever, but you must let up on me. I can't take your constant pulling me apart and pointing out my faults."

I was eagerly absorbing all the guilt, nodding *yes, yes, of course you're right.*

"No one knows my shortcomings better than I do. No one is is trying harder to overcome them." He looked so downcast that I was touched. "I love you and need you so," he said. "Just give me a little longer, and I know I'll be better."

He took my hand and held it as tenderly as he had done that first night years ago. Then we cried together and made more promises about a better future.

When he left the next morning for a business trip to Chicago, he said: "Darling, I know how hard this has been for you, and how much I have to make up to you. But, you know, Dr. Wolff is on your side always, except that he agrees with me that sometimes you press too hard on me at just the wrong time. So please, try not to kick me when I'm down. That's when I need you most."

I was totally worn out and repentant. I swore I'd be better for him in the future. I was persuaded that his progress depended on me. First thing on Monday morning, I looked up Dr. Wolff's telephone number. It was time that I met the man who was directing my fate. He could explain to me how I could best help Alan. His answering service took my name and number and said the doctor would call back.

"This is Dr. Wolff," he said when he returned my call several hours later. "What can I do for you?"

I told him I was a friend of Alan's and that it was urgent that I see him as soon as possible. He was very professional and distant on the phone, not reacting to my name at all.

"Tonight at six," he said.

He turned out to be a kindly looking man in his late fifties, and I felt immediately at ease with him. I again told him my name and the name of his patient (my lover), and waited for a flicker of response from the man who had been seeing Alan for three years.

"Ah, yes, I do remember him now. The architect. Yes, indeed, I did see him, but that was only for two months. I would say it was about two and a half years ago. That's why it took me so long to recall him. How can I help you?"

I was stunned. For three years I had loved and trusted a man who was admittedly sick, but who assured me that he was getting treatment that would make him well. How many times had he looked into my eyes and told me how good Dr. Wolff was for him, and how right I was to have urged him to undergo treatment? "Just bear with me a little longer, darling," he had said. "Dr. Wolff thinks I'm doing fine." And just two days before, sobbing and begging me for another chance, he had quoted Dr. Wolff as saying I should be easier on him, more understanding about his problems.

I poured out the story of the last three years. I told Dr. Wolff about my marriage, about Karen and David, about my struggle to earn a living for myself and to take care of my daughter's future. I told him about my love for and trust in Alan, about our quarrels, about how I hated what it was doing to me.

If I was stunned, so was he.

"My dear young woman," he said, shaking his head sadly, "from the few times I saw Alan, I knew that he was a deeply disturbed man. I told him that and that he would need intensive therapy. Then I never saw him again."

I was reeling from the enormous lie I had been forced to live all these years. I felt that once again, my world had caved in.

"You are young," the doctor said. "Your life is ahead of you. I advise you not to see Alan again. He is dangerous. He certainly hasn't done you any good. I'm afraid from what I know and from what you tell me that he can't be a husband to anyone now. It's doubtful that he can ever be."

I went home and told David I wasn't feeling well. I retched until I felt my insides coming apart. Then I went to bed. Goodbye dream, goodbye happy ending, goodbye my love. Goodbye everything.

Chapter 19

HOW MANY YEARS does it take to learn that you can't twist reality around to make things turn out your way? It took me decades, nearly the first half of my life.

I would have gone on that way for the rest of my life, fighting and suffering every inch of the way, if I had not finally reached bottom and been forced to remake myself. My luck and my tragedy was Karen. She had begun as the pretty baby of my dreams and had turned my life into a nightmare—because of what she was and because of the person I was. She became the instrument of my self-realization. I have her to thank for forcing me to make a new life out of the old lives that failed.

In the first years after Alan, my children and my work were all I had to sustain me. There were men, yes, but I allowed no man to get close to me emotionally. I sought friendships with single women and couples. I made as many friends as I could. Never mind that many of them were people who contributed nothing to my life except their physical presence. I considered myself lucky that anyone wanted to be my friend.

My children alone gave me moments of real happiness. I took such pride in David, who was growing up to be a strong, self-reliant, sane young man. He, it seemed, had weathered the storms and traumas of adolescence. How, I don't know, considering the mess his mother had made of her life. But I could look on him then, as now, as one of the blessings of my life.

I derived pleasure from being with Karen, when I wasn't wrestling with the problems she created just by living. When I was able to forget my anxieties about her (which were often anxieties about myself and how I could deal with her), I could participate happily in her life as she led it when she was at home with me.

I enjoyed seeing her reactions when she was faced with small dilemmas, taking the easy way out of difficult situations—"Forget about it"—expressing definite ideas about what she wanted, who she liked.

Karen always loves being sociable. The first question asked of a visitor she isn't familiar with is: "Do you know my daddy?" To an answer of no, she goes on to: "You know my mommy and my brother." She has the picture straight: the visitor knows the people in this apartment, not the people in her father's apartment.

To me: "Go to the kitchen and make the dinner. I will stay here with this person," whereupon she starts to remove the guest's shoes. He or she will have to stay and amuse Karen.

"David sleeps in that bed. I sleep with my mother. You stay and sleep in that bed over there." There is no way that vistior is going to be allowed to depart.

It's all done with signs. It's like living with Harpo Marx.

While I sit back and laugh at Karen's antics, it seems that she is not so different from other people. She wants happy endings, a world where everyone is nice and everything is beautiful. It makes me glad that she has something positive in her life, an idea of her kind of perfection which she sometimes achieves.

One of the continuing threads in Karen's life had been her father. He had never been able to cope with going out in the world and finding help for her, the way I did. But privately, at home, he was devoted to her. In her teens, as well as when she was a baby, he was loving and patient. He worked with her even when he was too impatient to work well with his son. Karen adored him. When she was home for vacations, he would arrive at my apartment each night after work and stay with Karen until eleven, watching television, reading with her, listening to her recount the day's adventures.

During Karen's late teens her father and I had shelved all discussion of a divorce. He seemed to cling to the myth that we were still a family, even though I knew I never was and never could be the kind of wife he should have. He needed a very different kind of woman. The more I saw of him in the years following our separation, the more I saw that he deserved happiness in his life, as I did in mine. He, too, had had a terrible heartache. How great a blow to male pride it must be to recognize that you are the father of a defective child, no matter for what reason. Women, I think, can bounce back from that kind of tragedy and get on with doing what must be done. For a man, it is a defeat.

I wanted not to feel guilty about him, but I felt guilty for years, once I had gotten over my rage against him. Then I just added that guilt to guilt about Karen, and the guilt about my mother's death that I never seemed able to shake.

Once more, when I was going to be in San Antonio on business, I called him to say that I could easily go to Juarez, Mexico and get a divorce. There was only silence at the other end of the line.

"It's been six years now. I really think we ought to do it, Richard."

He didn't say anything.

"Are you there?"

"Yes."

"Well, what do you have to say?"

"Nothing . . ."

My friends asked me why I didn't get a divorce anyway. They had seen the shedding of husbands and wives accomplished in a flash, and many had gone through it themselves.

I heard it often: "My dear, I divorced ———— and got a wonderful settlement." My husband had nothing to settle on me. Until Alan, there were no arms waiting for me to fall into. Somehow this last thread binding me to him—the marriage that still existed on a piece of paper—gave me a sense of belonging even yet to my long-ago dream life.

Then one day he called. "Do you remember what we were talking about a year or so ago?"

I couldn't imagine what he was talking about.

He could hardly get the words out: "About the divorce."

"Yes, I remember."

"Well, I think you were right. Maybe it's a good idea, and we should do it."

I knew he'd been seeing someone on and off for a couple of years. Now I supposed he wanted to marry her.

"Fine," I told him, "but I want you to know that your financial contribution to the children has to go on exactly as it always has."

He was contributing to David's support, and he had also been paying a considerable amount toward Karen's tuition, which was increasing every year.

"Of course nothing will change," he said. "Everything will go on just the way it was."

"I've been talking to Leonard about the divorce." Leonard and his wife were friends from the early days of our marriage, and Leonard, a lawyer, had kept up his friendship with Richard, though not with me.

"Leonard says that since we've been separated so long, it would be silly to spend a lot of money on legal fees and hire two lawyers, especially when we already have such financial obligations to Karen. He's agreed to act for both of us."

"If you two can agree on a settlement," Leonard told me on the phone, "whatever the unwritten agreement is, I'll put it down on paper for you. It's a friendly divorce. We just want to be sure it's all spelled out about Karen, so you won't have any worries in the future. I'll have a lawyer for you to sign the papers, but I'll do all the work."

Leonard had never been so cordial, and I needed those soothing words because until then I hadn't really come to grips with the finality of getting a divorce after all those years. I hadn't realized what an emotional thing it would be for me. We were going to put down on paper in legal language what was going to become of Karen, who would hold the responsibility for her. It seemed so ominous and so final. Even more disturbing was that I was finally being cut loose. There would be no husband anywhere, no person who theoretically wanted me, even if I didn't want him. It was a kind of rejection, and it hit me hard.

When I went to Leonard's office to discuss the divorce, everyone was sitting around laughing and talking and eating corned beef sandwiches. Whatever Leonard said, I nodded yes to. After all, we were all friends together, eating our sandwiches and writing up a friendly divorce settlement.

"Now," said Leonard, "when it comes to custody of the children, that's just a formality. The custody will be in Helene's name, of course."

I nodded yes. David was starting college, and Karen hadn't lived at home for ten years; so it didn't seem to be saying much that I would have custody of them. It didn't occur to me that if by an unlikely chance, Karen were ever without a school, her father legally had no obligation to take part in caring for her. Her home was with me. He wasn't obliged to share the emotional and physical demands of fetching and returning her to school, or keeping her during part of her vacations.

Then we came to the money part. It ended up with Richard agreeing to pay a fixed sum of money each year toward Karen's tuition and to continue contributing to David's support. There was no mention of who would pay Karen's medical and dental bills, her clothing and transportation—things her father had always taken care of. It wasn't mentioned, and it turned out that it was to be me.

But I nodded yes to everything. I wasn't worried about tuition. For the first time, there was a chance that the state would absorb the entire financial burden for Karen.

In 1972 Geraldo Rivera's television exposé of Willowbrook, a large New York State institution for the handicapped, had spurred the movement to make changes in the state's method of giving aid to disabled persons. An aid to the disabled act was passed, whereby the state of New York would assume the financial care of handicapped persons over the age of twenty-one if they were residing in a public or private New York institution.

I was sure I could find a place for Karen in New York State, so it wouldn't matter about her father's contribution. I was lulled into thinking that everything was going to be all right. No one pointed out that friendly agreements are different from legally binding documents, that the fixed sum to be paid by Karen's father might not, in a few years, cover more than a fraction of the increased cost of caring for her, should no state aid be forthcoming. At the time all that seemed impossible. I was too busy feeling unhappy about finally being a divorced woman to think rationally about what all this meant for my future.

Shortly after our divorce was final, Richard remarried, and I saw the devotion of years gradually change. The little girl who had seemed so important to him took a different place in his life. Perhaps, after all, he had grown weary of his obligations to her, and in spite of his love for her, he sought relief by removing himself from her.

It struck me as a harsh decision, whatever the reason, and I railed against him for years. After all, I was as close to her as ever.

"Mrs. Brown," a lawyer once told me long after the divorce, "the court can order your ex-husband to pay a certain amount of money for the support of your child, but it cannot order him to love her."

A single woman at last, and truly adrift, I saw myself and Karen growing old together. There was still so much I wanted to do, so many parts of my dreams that had never had a chance to come true. I became determined to make up for some of my misfortunes through my work and through the satisfaction of having Karen settled permanently for the rest of her days. Then there might still be time for me to give something to myself.

Chapter 20

ℰ

Aᴏᴏ ᴀ ᴛᴇʀ ɪ ʜᴀᴅ ʙᴇᴇɴ associate editor for four years, my boss, the interior design editor, announced that she was retiring. Her job was the job I had dreamed of. I knew that I could do it, and that I deserved the chance. While I was planning and photographing stories, writing copy, and supervising assistant editors, I had learned to administer the department as efficiently as she had done. Now I wanted the title and the glory that went with it.

My career had become the driving force in my life. It was the one world where I felt absolutely self-confident, where I could achieve satisfaction. I needed my career to make up for the fact that I had so few satisfactions elsewhere, that I was facing more than ever the responsibility for Karen, that my son was leaving home for college, that Alan had destroyed the last shreds of my belief in romance, that my mother and father had died, and that Karen existed.

The politics of magazine publishing are such, however, it can't be assumed that a second-in-command automatically takes over when an opportunity arises. The editor of the magazine left me in suspense while he pondered possible candidates for the job held by my boss. I held my breath while my future was being decided.

Ironically, I was in a position to be qualified for the job solely because of Karen. The work during my four years at the magazine had been so horrendous, given the expectations and demands of my boss, that I might have given up long before. But the picture of Karen was always before me. I knew that if I were out of work for any reason, there was no way that Karen could be maintained at her school. So I kept at that job through long, hard years. I had to hope that someday my efforts would bring me the job that might give me financial security.

The editor delayed his decision. The interior design editor would be leaving within weeks, and still no successor had been named. Feverishly I tried to plan what I would do if someone else were brought in to fill the job I wanted so much. What if I were forced to resign and go elsewhere? The terrifying possibility of joblessness dogged my thoughts. I saw my child being cast out into the world because I didn't have an income with which to pay her tuition. I saw us living in a tiny apartment, as cheap as I could find, while I did—what?

By the time I was finally named interior design editor, my panic about the future had become obsessive. My worries about money were constant. This led me to make a serious mistake in my professional life, where for years I had been careful not to let Karen play any part. Instead of bargaining on my own merits for a raise to go along with the responsibilities of the new job, I begged for more money on the basis of having a crippled, retarded child to support.

The editor looked surprised at my revelation. "That's really too bad," he said. "I had no idea about your daughter." He didn't seem particularly moved by my pathetic story, though. "I'll see what I can do about more money."

I was so wrapped up in my anxieties that I didn't see that I could be dealt with not as a trained professional but as a person who couldn't afford to walk out if I didn't like the terms. I had a handicapped child to care for. The salary increase I was offered was a token. Raises usually aren't given out of sympathy. I accepted the job and the title which meant a lot to me, but it was the first and last time I used Karen as a substitute for my own abilities in my business life.

At least the job of interior design editor gave me something I had longed for all my life: a touch of glamour. I wasn't ever going to have the perfect suburban housewife life with a loving husband; that ideal had long since faded. What I did have was a kind of halfway star-studded life that I had yearned for.

Now, many years later, I am amused by the thrill I got from flying back and forth across the country in first-class luxury, meeting the famous people whose homes I photographed for the magazine. Sometimes I fancied myself a minor celebrity in my own right—the woman about whom people asked, "Who was that?"—as I swept through airports and hotel lobbies with a train of porters carrying my luggage. I could dine in Texas one week with oil millionaires and the next week in Hollywood with stars. I counted among my acquaintances film people, architects, writers, and artists. I had invitations to all the "right" parties with all the "right" people. It was a busy life. It was an empty life.

I didn't want a personal life in those years. I was traveling constantly, seeing new people and places, away from home almost half of every month. Often my suitcase wasn't completely unpacked before I left on another trip. When I was home, Friday nights found me at my apartment with an overstuffed briefcase of work to catch up on so I could leave the next week for Miami, for Phoenix, for Boston, San Francisco, Los Angeles, or Dallas.

There were always acquaintances to have dinner with, attractive men as escorts when I needed them, men I kept at arm's length. I never again wanted to hear a man say, "I've never felt this way about any woman before." I didn't want to be hurt again.

With Claudette alone I maintained a close personal relationship, that grew closer and warmer as years passed. Her kindness and love for Karen was boundless; her patience in listening to me was endless. Claudette alone knew the insecure and sometimes frightened person under the fashionable, self-assured facade I displayed in public. She knew the sources of my anguish. She was an exceptional friend.

For the rest of the world, I developed a dramatic style suitable for someone who was a star at last.

While performing my act for the general public, I was still deeply concerned about Karen's future. She had been at the school in Pennsylvania for nearly five years. She was happy there, but I didn't feel it was the right situation for her. I wanted her to have more educational and training opportunities. Perhaps I still hoped that some miracle would turn her into the normal daughter I never had.

When people said to me, "She's never going to go out in the world, she's never going to get married or have a job, so why do you worry so about giving her some kind of life?" I could only answer that she deserved everything in spite of her defects. She was a real person in her own right. The ties that bind us together are as strong as between any mother and daughter, and I was driven to find the best possible life for her.

The state of New York was developing a program of education and rehabilitation of handicapped children through the age of twenty-one, at which time, public and private facilities funded by the state would provide adult handicapped persons with a life that had some dignity and purpose. Self-contained villages for young adults opened, where residents did some kind of productive work, where they had a regular paycheck, where they lived as nearly normal lives as possible. There were also sheltered workshops where the handicapped who were able to live at home went each day to work or participate in a training program. There were all kinds of new schools appearing, and I was confident that I could find a worthwhile place for Karen in New York State. The state would then take over her tuition when she turned twenty-one, and she would have a secure home for the rest of her life. If something happened to me—and at forty, one begins to realize that life doesn't go on forever—Karen would have the security I wanted for her.

Several people recommended an upstate New York school which, they said, had an excellent reputation. Although the director told me that he was doubtful about taking a deaf child, he agreed to let me bring her to the school for a day and try her in one of the beginning classes so the staff could evaluate her.

The school was an enormous resort hotel that had been converted into a year-round residential school for teenage and adult handicapped persons. We were taken to a "classroom" where fifteen young people, all quite retarded and all apparently without much previous training, were being taught to make a bed. The teacher took me aside and told me that after the others had been called, she would have Karen try.

"Karen already knows how to make a bed. She's been doing it for years," I told her. The dedicated people at her first school in Pennsylvania had worked hard to teach Karen how to do things for herself around the house.

"Well . . ." The teacher looked at Karen dubiously. "We'll have to see for ourselves how much she knows and how responsive she is."

One by one the children went to the front of the room to try to make up a low bed. At first Karen was interested; bedmaking was something she understood. In a short time she was bored. She had quickly lost interest in watching all those kids try to make a bed she knew she could make.

"Is this a school?" Karen asked in sign language.

"Yes."

"Am I going to stay here and sleep here?"

"No."

"How long will we stay here? Do you love me? Are we going to eat lunch together?" She was going to get all the enjoyment possible out of her time with me.

"Karen, look at the teacher and fold your hands. Be quiet."

She sat up straight with hands folded—for a minute. Then she was pulling at my sleeve to get my attention.

"I told you to watch that teacher."

"Karen Brown." The teacher called her name at last.

I pointed and said: "Go up there and make that bed."

It wasn't easy for her to walk around the folding chairs to the front of the room.

"Go on, Karen; faster." I so wanted her to make a good impression.

She made the bed. She made it beautifully. When she finished, there was still a little piece of blanket sticking out, so she lifted the whole mattress with her crippled hands, standing on unsteady legs, and tucked it in neatly and perfectly.

I was as happy as if my child had graduated magna cum laude. I knew that, given the full use of her hands, she could do practically anything. She understood things like self-care and cleaning and working at easy tasks in a workshop. The fact that her hands and fingers didn't move properly alone prevented her from being completely independent of outside help.

We were asked to wait in the lobby until it was time for lunch. The lobby, a vast room that seemed to stretch for miles, was filled with dozens of sofas and chairs.

A voice boomed over the loudspeaker: "Lunch in ten minutes. Everybody get washed up for lunch."

Almost everyone who came through the lobby to get ready for lunch seemed to walk perfectly. No one was cerebral palsied like Karen. There were no wheelchairs, and no one appeared to be deaf. Many of them towered over Karen. I wondered if this was really the right place for her.

A teenage boy descended on us as we waited on a couch. "My mother died last year," he told me right away. "I miss her." Pointing to Karen, he said: "Are you her mother?"

"Yes."

"Well, my mother died, and my father and sister sent me here. They couldn't take care of me. This is a nice place."

Before I could answer, he turned his attention to Karen. "Are you coming to this school?"

Karen tried to read his lips but couldn't quite understand him.

The boy was puzzled. "Why doesn't she talk?"

"She can't hear."

"She's pretty. Is she coming here?"

"I don't know."

"If she's coming here, could she be my girl friend?"

I leaned back and laughed. It was so real and true to life. He had zeroed right in on her—the pretty new girl at school.

"We have dances here, you know," he said. "I bet she could dance."

Karen did love to dance. I pictured my daughter embarking on a life of romance in this huge place that looked like the resort it had once been.

"Could I hold her hand now?"

Karen's romantic idyll was suddenly interrupted by the loudspeaker. "The dining room is open."

About a hundred and fifty people started through the lobby toward the dining room at the far end. Karen's swain was caught up in the rush and disappeared.

"Karen, you go to the dining room for lunch." The director wanted her to be observed at mealtime without me. I had explained to him that she needed a soup bowl and a spoon, but otherwise she was capable of feeding herself, although a bit sloppily.

"Come with me," she said.

"No, you go alone."

"You wait for me here." Karen would never refuse food. Eating was one of the great pleasures of her life.

I watched her walk the length of the lobby, around sofas and chairs, and into the dining room. I didn't know where she was going, but I knew that she could find a seat for herself.

I was given a sandwich in the director's office and had scarcely finished when Karen came bursting into the room, tearing the napkin from around her neck.

(160)

She looked at me as if to say, *Aha, I found you. You tried to run out on me; but I caught you.*

"Let's leave," she said. "Let's go to the car."

"Not now," I told her. "You sit quietly while this man"— I indicated the director—"and I talk."

"Karen did well in the classroom situation," he told me. "The supervisor said she ate well too."

Of course she did. No handicap ever kept Karen from a good meal.

"I'll sit down with my staff and evaluate her," he said. "We have six applicants and only four places. I'm not convinced that this is the right place for Karen, and we'd be doing her an injustice to take her if she would be out of her element."

I agreed, silently. The people seemed too self-sufficient, and the distances were so vast. Still, if he thought she might fit in, I would send her. The school's program was just what I wanted for her. It wasn't far from home, and in a year, when she was twenty-one, the state would pay the tuition.

"I'll let you know in a week or ten days, Mrs. Brown."

Karen was already at the door when we stood up, eager to get out to the car and be on the road alone with her mother.

I took her back to her school in Pennsylvania, confident that she had performed well and would be accepted. Ten days later, she was refused. It was a disappointment but one I could handle. Perhaps I had blinded myself to the real difficulties of Karen's handicaps. To me, the fact that she could brush her teeth and walk about, dress and undress herself, and eat by herself was so constantly exciting that I blocked out the knowledge that she could do none of those things very well. Her interest in the world around her, her efforts to read and communicate through sign language and lip reading, often made me forget how limited her intelligence really was.

Next I applied to a school in the Catskills, on the border of New York and Pennsylvania. It was a brand-new private school, a former summer camp that the owners were in the process of converting into a facility for adult handicapped persons. Karen was accepted—with a tuition of $675 a month. It was settled that she would start at the beginning of December. I looked back on the agony of finding her a school the first time and thought how easy it had become.

I called Karen's father. "I've found a new school for Karen in New York. I'm picking her up in Pennsylvania at the end of November to take her to the new place. Will you come with me?"

It semed important that the school know that she wasn't being abandoned, that both her parents were there to support her.

He said: "I can't do it. I'll be away on vacation."

I could barely control my rage. I remembered vividly all the years we had never taken a vacation. Never mind, I screamed inside myself, I'll do it alone. I have to do everything myself!

When I arrived at the school in Pennsylvania, I could see that Karen was uneasy. Her lifetime of possessions were all packed up neatly in a couple of suitcases. She knew that something important was happening to her. It wasn't a day-long expedition with her mother or a few exciting weeks at home in New York.

"Mrs. Brown," the headmistress said, "I don't know how we can part with her. We understand why, but it's terribly hard. We loved her."

Everyone was so falsely cheerful that it was almost unbearable. Karen and the other girls knew that it wasn't "Goodbye, school; I'm going home to sleep with my mother."

It was Goodbye, school, period.

As we drove away, Karen looked back at her friends bundled up in the late-November cold in front of the house where she had nestled for five years. What had I done to her, cutting her loose from a familiar, comfortable life? If the future plans didn't work out, I had nowhere to turn. Karen was twenty. Her adjustment to a new way of life was going to be harder for her.

Everything seemed to be getting harder for me, too. I felt the sharp clutch of anxiety building in my chest, the constant reminder of my lack of serenity. It was with me through the Friday night rush-hour traffic driving home to Manhattan.

Chapter 21

ⱱ

KAREN AND I came back to my empty apartment, both of us depressed and disheartened. David was away at college, and I had been out of town for the two weeks before my trip to Pennsylvania. I had only spent the night there before picking up Karen. The place had the cold, deserted feel that settles on a home when no one has been there for a long time.

Saturday we were going to spend getting packed and ready. Sunday morning I was driving her upstate to the new school.

"Wash my hair. Put it in rollers." Karen perked up a little after she'd checked out the apartment for new additions, changes in furniture, the clothes in my closet.

"Where's my daddy?" That was a question I didn't have

an answer for. "Am I going back to my school? How many days?"

I sat her down and showed her a folder about the new school.

"You're going to this school." She looked nervously at the pictures and then at me. The new school didn't look like the one she knew and loved.

"You'll love the new school. It's fun." I clapped my hands. "They will love you," and I hugged her. "The school will love you and you will read and write and speak. You will weave at a loom."

She seemed to like the idea of doing these things.

She held up ten fingers. "I don't want to go for ten days."

"You're going in one day."

Karen screwed up her face for make-believe crying, the tears that flow when things aren't going just her way.

"Look," I said, "just forget about crying. You smile."

She sat there looking at me with a fixed, forced smile on her face and the tears running down her cheeks.

"Karen, smile. No more tears. Forget about crying and look at your new clothes."

That dried her tears immediately. Aside from food, there was nothing she liked better than new clothes. I had bought a whole new wardrobe for her. At her other school I had supplied her with regulation clothes: dark-colored skirts, plain tops, white knee socks. No school, I had discovered, was going to maintain her the way I would. Her clothes, her skin, her hair—none of them was of overriding importance to a school staff which had to deal with forty girls with various handicaps.

But for her new school, I indulged myself. It was like sending her away to college, the start of her adult life. Playing this game, I bought her all the things a mother would buy to send her daughter off to college: dresses, skirts, blouses, bathrobe and slippers, nightgowns, underwear, a pocketbook, shoes, and ribbons for her hair.

She tried on everything.

"Is this for me?" pointing in delight to a new dress. "And this? And this?"

"Yes, all of it."

In front of a full-length mirror, wearing a new dress, Karen looked over her shoulder at the back, admired the front view, then kissed me to show how happy she was. Then she was pulling that one off and choosing the next thing to try on. Saturday was filled with activity, Saturday night a time of exhaustion.

"Where is my daddy?" Karen was ready for bed, tired, cranky.

I told her wearily that he wasn't coming. "Go to sleep, Karen."

Worn out by the excitement and travel of the past two days, Karen cried herself to sleep.

I couldn't sleep, wondering how it was all going to turn out for us.

The school, set against a background of bare winter trees, snowy hills, and gray sky, was desolate beyond words. I had seen it before in the summer through leafy branches, with groups of people in the distance sitting around on sunny lawns. I never dreamed that the camplike atmosphere could change into what I now saw before me. Even Karen was a little taken aback at the sight of the grim administration building looming up in front of us.

The road winding up to the school was icy and the space at the foot of the steps was an expanse of churned up, slippery mud. When we went in to meet the director, Karen was clinging to me. She was unnaturally quiet.

Please don't let her make a bad impression, I prayed.

"Is this my school? I want to go home."

To the head of the school I said, "Karen is a little nervous. She'll settle down."

I hoped that wasn't a look of doubt on his face.

"I'm sure she'll be fine, Mrs. Brown. I'll have one of the girls take you over to Karen's house."

The housemother was a young woman who looked like a college student.

"Of course, we're still in the process of setting up our facilities," she told me as we struggled with Karen's suitcases and Karen down a muddy, icy incline to the house where Karen would live.

"I'm sure it's going to be very pleasant." I was looking at a wooden, barracks-like building that no one could do much to improve.

"This is the main living room." The housemother opened a door, and I was confronted with a glimpse of the reality of Karen's future life. Seated around the room—quiet, passive, indifferent to us—were Karen's fellow residents, women in their thirties, forties, and fifties. Many of them were much older than I was. They were all retarded to one degree or another, and they weren't pleasant to look at. Karen seemed like an infant next to them. Barely five feet tall, she was surrounded by full-grown, mature, grayhaired women who looked at us vacantly for a moment and then looked away.

It was all I could do to keep from taking Karen by the hand and leading her to the car, back to Manhattan and my apartment, where at least she would have me. She'd always been in a school with girls her own age. I had watched them all grow up together. I had never seen women like this, who had perhaps spent their whole lives in huge state institutions and had now been placed in this facility in the course of the state's efforts to empty overcrowded state institutions. This was to be Karen's adult life which, I had been thinking, was like sending my daughter to college.

I helped Karen unpack her new clothes in the big dormitory, which had low wooden partitions dividing up the sleeping areas. I explained to the housemother about Karen's sign language, what kinds of things were important to her, what she liked and disliked.

"Don't worry, Mrs. Brown. We'll take good care of her."

"I'm going to leave now," I told the housemother. "Karen is going to be very upset today, and the sooner I get out of here, the better it will be for her."

I gave Karen a hurried kiss and left without giving her a chance to cry and hold onto me.

It was four o'clock on a darkening winter afternoon when I left Karen at her new school. It was the grayest, most dismal day of the year, and possibly of my life. A few snowflakes started to fall. When I turned the car in the driveway, I made the mistake of looking back toward Karen's dormitory. I saw an anguished little face pressed against a window, Karen sobbing as I drove away.

Her image stayed with me along the thruway. It still haunted me when I returned to my apartment, which was still littered with boxes and bags from Karen's new clothes. It was still with me as I put my head on my pillow that night.

What have I done to her? I kept thinking. I shouldn't have done it. What's the matter with me that I can't take care of her at home? How can I let her stay in that kind of place?

Those first days, I was a wreck. I called the school after a week. "Karen is fine," I was told, but I didn't believe it. How could she be fine in a place like that? I had committed her to a life that didn't have anything to recommend it.

I called the second week and the third. "Karen is doing just fine, Mrs. Brown. She's behaving well. She seems to be adjusting. We do have to drive her back and forth to the dining room because it's too icy for her to walk, but otherwise the housemother doesn't report any problems."

I couldn't face the fact that everything was all right, that Karen was getting along without me.

Suddenly it was Christmas week, and for the first time in my life, I was going to be completely alone for the holidays. Usually Karen and David were with me, filling the days with activity; but this year it was too soon to bring Karen home after changing schools. Every acquaintance I had in the city was away on vacation or with parents or relatives. My brother, Larry, whom I didn't see frequently anyhow, was off somewhere; Claudette was visiting relatives in Canada. Even my son was away. David walked into the house one snowy night, picked up his bathing suit, and said, "So long, I'm driving to Florida with my roommate for the holidays," and was gone.

Having nothing else to worry about, I worried about him through a sleepless night, waiting for the phone to ring. There was no way, I was convinced, that he could drive for twenty-four hours. and end up alive in Florida. Before he left, I had tucked a paper into his pocket: "In case of emergency, call. . . ." No call came.

I faced the realization that not only did I have no one to be with for Christmas, but that I faced years of nothing and no one. I was really independent for the first time in my life—and I couldn't handle it. I roamed around the apartment awash in a flood of overwhelming loneliness. The phone was silent. There was no trip scheduled for me until early January. My work at the office was caught up. Somehow I couldn't see myself working through the holidays at home or at the magazine's empty offices.

When the phone rang, I pounced on it.

"What are you doing Christmas Eve?" It was the cheerful

voice of my friend, Jean. She and her husband were long-time business and social friends. "Harry and I are driving out to our house in the country for a few days, and if you don't have any other plans, please come with us. Bring David along if he's home."

"David's away. I was planning to stay around here and catch up on things." I really wanted so much to be with someone, but I was ashamed to admit that I had nothing to do, no family to be with. Then instinctively I thought: "I can't go away. What if Karen needs me?"

Jean said firmly: "We'd love to have you. We can pick you up at noon tomorrow."

I thought again. I had to take the school at its word; Karen was all right.

"I'd love to come," I told Jean. "See you tomorrow."

It turned out to be a wonderful time. The house was private and snug, facing a lake, and the winter winds blew around us as we curled up in front of the fireplace to laugh and talk and exchange gifts. Slowly in the couple of days I was there, I began to unwind. I took solitary walks along the shore. I thought a lot. I was, I decided, a lucky lady after all. Karen was settled at last. David was growing up and turning into a fine young man. My job filled me with satisfaction. Maybe now I could relax and start to think about myself and my future.

"This has been a wonderful holiday for me," I told Jean. I was feeling so good that I couldn't wait to get to work on the future.

I returned to Manhattan peaceful, relieved, happy, optimistic. I called the school. Karen was still doing all right. At the beginning of January, I left on a cross-country trip that would take most of the month.

"Why don't you come live out here in California?" several

friends asked. "You love it here. You could certainly find some interesting work to do."

Yes, I thought I might just do that. There were a lot of things I wanted to do. I wanted to take a trip to England to see Margaret. Once Karen was twenty-one and that $675-a-month tuition bill was off my shoulders, I'd have some money for the first time. I was full of plans.

As I walked into my apartment after that long trip, before I even had a chance to look at the mail that had accumulated, the phone was ringing.

"The people at the school have been trying to reach you." It was Richard. "When they couldn't, they called me." He sounded annoyed. I felt a little twinge of panic.

"What did they want? Is something wrong with Karen?" In spite of leading a life precariously upright on two unsteady legs, Karen had never had a serious injury in any of her falls. Lots of scars and bruises. But I had a morbid fear that she would really hurt herself one day.

"She's OK, but they say they can't keep her. It isn't working out the way they'd hoped. She's the only one who can't walk alone to the dining room and manage her boots and coat. They can't keep anyone who isn't self-sufficient."

"They can't mean that! They told me she was getting on fine. I talked to them just before I went away. There's got to be some mistake."

"No mistake. I talked to the director myself. Now I don't know what you're going to do about this. . . ."

What was he saying? He didn't know what *I* was going to do?

". . . but you'd better call them right away."

In the mail was a letter from the school:

We have come to be very fond of Karen, but we · have decided that it is impossible for us to keep her. She has not adjusted to life here as we had hoped. Her deafness and physical handicaps require more supervision than we are able to provide. This makes it necessary for us to ask you to come and take her out of school as soon as possible. Please let us know when you will be arriving so that we can have Karen packed and ready to leave.

I had no idea what I was going to do. I couldn't understand why they were sending her away after the assurances I had been given. Should I bring her home to stay? Should I have her with me and give her nothing that she needed? Put her in a state institution after all? It was out of the question.

Since I didn't know what to do, I did nothing. I went to bed. I didn't call the school; I didn't call anyone. Who could help me now? I lay on my bed and sobbed. My month and a half of happiness and serenity, my plans for the future, had vanished with a phone call and a letter.

Having no one else to call who had the remotest connection with my problem, I called Ann Coleman. She was a New York State social worker at a facility for the handicapped and retarded in Greenwich Village. It was a half-way house between the large state institutions and the smaller institutions the state was encouraging. She'd been assigned to me by the state to keep track of Karen's file in preparing her eligibility papers for aid to the disabled.

"Mrs. Coleman, I'm calling you because I don't know where else to turn."

"Don't get upset, Mrs. Brown," she said when I had given her the gist of my problem. "We'll work something out."

I flew to her office. I shelved my own life for a while, so that she and I could set about planning Karen's life—once more.

Chapter 22

ॐ

"DON'T WORRY," Ann Coleman said soothingly, "they're not going to put her out in the street. I'm going to call the school for you and tell them they'll have to keep her until you can make other arrangements."

"But will they do that? They wrote me weeks ago, and I haven't even spoken to them yet myself."

"I refer a lot of people to them, and I'm in a position to make some suggestions. They'll listen to me."

Ann was calm and efficient. She seemed to be dedicated in her job. I don't know what she was doing for any of her other cases, but she dealt with Karen's as if it were her only problem to solve. And in helping Karen, she helped me when I needed it the most.

After all these years, I was finally falling apart. My anxiety was constant. It was a crushing weight on my chest. Panic was ruling my life. I sat in her office day after day, shaking and crying, as we tried to find a solution. I was unable to take another step on my own, while this intelligent, hard-working young woman sat across the desk, trying to keep me under control.

Between tearful conversations, I'd check in at my office from the pay phone in the hall. My secretary needed an answer to a letter. The editor wanted me in his office at three for an editorial meeting. Somebody wondered if I was free for lunch the next day.

"I'll be there for the meeting," I'd say. "We'll take care of the letter when I get back. Call _____ back and tell him I can't make it for lunch. I'll call him when I'm free."

Having dealt for the moment with my professional life, I went back to the shambles of my private life, which no one in my office except my boss was aware of.

"What's the next step, Ann? I've seen most of the schools in New York State. Some of the possible ones have already refused her. The rest won't even consider Karen with her handicaps."

"Well, her present school will keep her another two weeks or so. Then if we haven't found anything, I've arranged for her to come here. We have a six weeks' respite program where we take children whose parents are ill or have an emergency and can't keep them at home for a while."

I said, not quite believing it: "Surely we'll be able to find a place for her in the next two months."

"And I can probably get her stay here extended to take us up to June. There are always camps she can go to, and that would give us until September."

Karen's immediate problem had been coped with, but there was one more emergency: me. I was barely functioning. The shock of losing the peace I thought I had found when Karen seemed to be settled for life had done something terrible to me. When I wasn't in Ann's office, I was spending my days walking the street of New York, crying without letup. I was hiding in my office behind closed doors because I couldn't bear to face anybody.

"I'm going to lose my job if this continues," I told Ann. "I have a creative job. I have to create beautiful rooms and write copy and meet deadlines. I have to be free to travel and be pleasant to all kinds of people. And I've never been so depressed."

"Have you considered getting help?"

"I've spoken to my doctor. I told him what was happening and he said: 'I don't know what to tell you. . . . You have real troubles.' He gave me some tranquilizers which only sedated me. My life is one of constant worry about my two children, of trying to support them and keep up my work. I don't have a social life any more. I wonder why I keep trying. I just can't see my way out of it."

"We're going to find something for Karen, I'm certain."

"It's not just Karen, you know. It's me, too. I'm going around and around in circles. I feel like a worn-out old woman. I think about suicide all the time."

And I *had* thought about it often enough: during the long nights, on lonely, tearful walks through dark Manhattan streets, shut up in my office, the past, present, and future becoming bleaker day by day.

"I think," said Ann, "that you really have to find some professional help for yourself."

Of course I'd thought about that, too. Years before, after my mother died, when my grief over her was at its peak, I had gone to a psychiatrist. I'd found the experience unsatisfactory. Also I didn't have the money it took. Nevertheless, I knew I was about as close to the end of my mental and physical rope as I could get and still be alive.

"I guess I should try to see someone," I said to Ann. "But I don't know who to go to. I can't just pick some doctor's name out of the yellow pages."

"Would you like me to see if I can find one for you? My husband is a doctor. He can ask some of his colleagues."

"Yes, please."

I stopped thinking about how much it was going to cost. I wanted to live and go on and be well for myself and for Karen and David. I wanted help to get me through this terrifying time.

A week later I had a call from Ann: "Here's the name of a doctor. He's expecting to hear from you."

"I can see you immediately," he told me when I called. "Can you make it today?" He sounded so kind and gentle. He would make everything all right.

I practically ran to his office. I was remembering Dr. Wolff, wise and understanding, a father figure who would solve all my problems.

"Come in, Mrs. Brown." I was ushered into the office by a young man who might have passed for a medical student.

Depressed as I was, I could see how ridiculous this was going to be. He was a very young man who couldn't possibly help me.

"Why don't you tell me something about your immediate problems?"

I took a deep breath. I wanted to dismiss him at once, but I couldn't start running around to different psychiatrists until I found one who fit my movie image of what a psychiatrist should be. So I sat and talked for an hour about everything, tearfully, desperately pouring out all the anguish

I had gone through because of Karen, how I was all alone and I didn't know what to do.

He leaned back in his chair with the tips of his fingers together. I wondered if doctors learned that in medical school.

"I'd like to see you again in a few days' time," he said. "I'll evaluate what you've told me and consider what might be a course of treatment for you and what we can realistically expect from it." He thought for a moment and then said: "Can you come back in two days?"

I could, but I couldn't let it go at that—not I. I had to protect myself from being disappointed by this youth disguised as a doctor when it turned out that he couldn't do anything for me.

"Doctor, I can come back, but I have to tell you that I am practically penniless. I don't know how I'm going to be able to pay you. That's the first thing. Second, I don't really believe in psychiatry. I've seen a lot of people in all kinds of therapy and analysis, and I've never seen one I thought was any better off after it than before."

He smiled. It was that kind of smile psychiatrists put on when they know something you don't. "We'll talk about your reservations about therapy when I've had another talk with you. As for the money, think about this: You've managed to find money to pay for everything you've thought was important—your daughter's school and care, your son's schooling, whatever you thought was necessary for your professional life. Dn't you think it's time you felt you were important enough to do something for? If you think that getting help for yourself is important enough, you'll manage, whether you come to me or go to another doctor."

I went away thinking he was being too harsh on me, and was back two days later for another hour of nonstop talk.

I threw out everything, all the agonies of my life: being alone; the loss of my parents; the terrible struggle with Karen and not being able to cope any more; problems with my job; problems with my son; recurring aches and pains and illnesses that doctors always told me were psychosomatic; the anxiety I was filled with every waking moment; my marriage; the hurt inflicted by the men in my life: Richard, Paul, Alan, and others; just being single and alone, always alone.

I ended up feeling utterly discouraged. When I laid out all my woes end to end, they seem to stretch from the doctor's office over the horizon into infinity. It seemed more hopeless than ever.

"As I told you last time, Doctor, I don't see around me any good examples of people in analysis, but I'm desperate enough to take some drastic measures. Whatever treatment you think best is worth a try."

"I think I can promise you some improvement, but—"

"But," I interrupted him, "I want it to be clear that I'll only embark on some course of treatment if there's a cutoff point of six months. I don't have time to lie on a couch for the next five or six years and free-associate. I have an immediate problem, and I have to get it solved. If you can help me do that, I'll be your patient."

I figured that my life was worth the six months I had set as the limit. If the therapy saved my life, it was worth the loan I'd have to take. If it didn't save my life, it wouldn't matter much.

Another smile from the doctor as he said: "Twice a week, I think, is the absolute minimum for any kind of sensible treatment. You should see me three times a week, but I understand the financial problem."

"All right," I said. "I can come twice a week. How much will it cost?"

He told me. Perhaps I had thought he was going to give me a special rate because my story was so pathetic.

Later he said to me: "You have to ask for what you are worth. You have to make people who want your services pay you properly. You're a talented woman. Don't sell yourself short just so people will like you, or because you think so little of yourself that you feel you have to give yourself away at bargain rates."

I didn't understand that at the time. I was still floundering around at the mercy of the system in business that says women don't really deserve as much money as a man, and anyhow, a divorced woman probably has alimony or a rich boyfriend in the background supplying all the money she needs.

So I swallowed the news about the doctor's fee and agreed to his twice-a-week schedule.

"The first thing I want you to do," I told him as I took charge of my treatment, "is give me something to get me out of this depression and back in shape. I want to be dead most of the time. Sometimes it's only a question of figuring out how to do it."

"I can give you some medication," he said, "and I want you to follow my instructions for dosage exactly. Let me know how it works, and I'll see you next week."

The medication worked. I had periods of no anxiety, and I even felt alive again, after feeling like death for so long. It was a small miracle that I had managed to uncover two people capable of holding me together. Just their existence made me feel stronger, even, possibly, able to move forward. I still didn't quite comprehend that Ann Coleman and the doctor weren't able themselves to stick together the shattered pieces of myself. Only I could do that.

Chapter 23

ॐ

IN MARCH I used some of my newfound strength to ask Richard for help. "Karen is being moved back to the city to a temporary school this week." I told him what the immediate plans for her were. "I just can't make that trip upstate to get her. You have to do it for me and for her."

I had been so full of hope about the school, so happy for that brief period when I thought she was settled, and so destroyed when she was handed back to me, that I knew I couldn't drive up to that front door again and face the director and the housemother.

"All right," he said. "I'll drive up on the weekend. You call and make the arrangements."

I had been prepared to scream at him if he had hesitated for one second. I was almost disappointed that I didn't get the chance.

When I told my doctor, he asked: "Why do you get so much enjoyment from your rages at your former husband? Why do you need that drama of forcing things to a head and then tearing apart the people who don't do things your way?"

"It's not a question of drama. Those people have to help me. They're giving me all the responsibility. I have a right to get angry when they don't act as they should."

"You mean, as you *think* they should. You're not just getting angry when someone doesn't fit in with some plan of yours. You get filled up with a rage that's a symptom of something deeper—the unfairness of life maybe—not just what this person or that is doing."

"Life has been very unfair to me; I shouldn't have to have all this responsibility. Why shouldn't I be in a rage when everyone always lets me down. I don't want to have to suffer through all this by myself."

"When you understand yourself—"

"Look," I said, "what I don't need is a lot of abstract psychiatrist's talk. I know you're a very smart man, but what I need now is to keep the comparative calmness I've acquired in the past few weeks, so I can handle Karen's problem. You're keeping me afloat, but once she's settled, I can float alone."

"OK," he said, "if Karen is so important to your well-being, let's see that you get her settled."

"Of course she's important! She's the most important thing in my life. Everything I do is for her."

"Is that right?" he said. I wasn't sure how he meant it,

whether it was sarcasm or a question about the correctness of my attitude toward Karen.

When I saw her again, brought home by her father on Saturday to start school in the city on Monday, my heartache vanished. Of course it was right. Confronted by the reality of her, laughing and loving, delighted to be with me, I felt that someone had put a soothing lotion on an open wound.

There were constant questions, more new clothes. The beautiful wardrobe of a few months before had disappeared, leaving suitcases crammed with unfamiliar dresses belonging to someone twice her size.

"Tell me about your school." It seemed to me that it couldn't have been a good experience for her if they had wanted her gone so quickly. She rummaged through the suitcase and brought out some cards with new words she had been taught. We went through them one by one and she gave the sign for each, telling me who this person was and what that word meant.

We came to a card that said, "Robert." At the sight of it, Karen jumped up and threw her arms around my neck. Whoever Robert was, a teacher or a boy at the school, Karen had obviously found someone she adored. She carried the card around with her the whole weekend and slept with it on her pillow. I felt good that her months at the school hadn't been as terrible as I had pictured them. A simple diet of love sustained her; the clothes and people and bare trees didn't make any difference to her.

I remembered something the doctor had said when we were talking about my feelings about her school and what kind of life I wanted for her.

"Remember," he said, "that Karen is neither as happy or as unhappy as you and I are about things, about the places she lives, about the course of her life. Of course you want her to be comfortable; certainly, as you've said, no child deserves to live in conditions a person would reject for a pet, but what Karen sees through her eyes is not at all what we see."

When I started to protest and say that she loved pretty clothes and going out in the world, he reminded me that Karen had a different frame of reference. The people she lived with were not, to her, "retarded" people; they were people just like her.

"Only *you* see them as old and retarded. Only you make the judgment that this dress is stylish and pretty and that one isn't. You have to stop pretending that she is really a normal person and learn to separate yourself from her. And in doing so, you will ease some of the suffering you have about her."

That kind of distance from Karen wasn't possible for me then. He was right, but I had to examine yet another school critically. I had to go down to Greenwich Village and see still another refuge among strangers for Karen.

The building that housed the school was new, institutional but clean and modern. Karen was going to have a chance to be thoroughly evaluated by speech and hearing therapists. Modern developments in therapy and equipment might make it possible for her to learn to hear certain sounds such as music and danger signals. The daytime situation gave me no bad feelings—except that the other residents were, of course, painful to see. Many of them had lived for years in institutions under conditions which had deprived them of love, learning, and care.

After Karen had been settled in the school for a few days, however, I began to see conditions that made me uneasy. On evening visits when the regular staff was gone, I would encounter half-naked old men in the hallways, little girls in their nightgowns sitting on the floor playing with dolls, and night attendants who seemed to be of a lower mentality than the residents. I tried not to see the laxness of the supervision, the staff that preferred to spend time in dark corners with each other instead of attending to the children.

It's only going to be for a few weeks, I kept telling myself. Ann is looking for a school, and she's going to find one. Remember what the doctor said: put all the bad things you see out of your mind.

Another miracle: we found a school in Brooklyn. It had a summer camp upstate where Karen could go in June and start at the school in the fall. Ann arranged an extension of her stay at the respite program until camp started.

Those other things weren't meant to be, I told myself. This is a far better situation for her. I should learn from this experience and never again be pessimistic about life.

I told the doctor how happy and excited I was. "I feel that I'm getting well," I told him. "Everything has changed. I feel so good. Maybe I won't be seeing you much longer."

"Maybe," he said. "I'm glad things are working out for Karen."

I had to go to Florida for four days and decided that when I got back, I'd bring Karen home for a weekend with me. She would have missed my almost daily visits while I was away. I returned home exhausted, in the first stages of flu, and by Friday night I knew I wouldn't be in any condition to pick her up the next morning and devote a weekend to entertaining her.

I'll call the school in the morning, I thought as I sank into a feverish sleep. She's not expecting me to come home, so she won't be disappointed.

I awoke on Saturday feeling very ill. I turned on the radio and dozed, absorbed in how terrible I felt.

"And now the news," came over the radio. National news, Nixon, Watergate, international news, Israel, Egypt, Russia.

Local news: "Yesterday at a state facility for the handicapped in Greenwich Village, three young women were abducted from their beds . . . the intruder was captured by police . . . is being arraigned on charges of. . . ."

I was wide awake, sitting up, dizzy with fever, practically suffocating from panic and anxiety. It can't be Karen, I thought. It can't. This can't happen to me. It happens in books, but you don't hear things like that about your own daughter over the radio.

A mother worries constantly that her daughter might be hurt or molested, whether the child is a normal child or one like mine, innocent and helpless, who can't speak or cry out, who can barely walk, and who is at the same time an attractive and mature young woman. My Karen was a grown-up baby taken care of half the time by people untrained for their work. And I had just heard that three girls at her school had been molested during the night.

I will not believe it was Karen, I said over and over to myself as I searched for the school's number. They would have called me if it had been Karen. It can't be her.

"This is Karen Brown's mother," I said to the woman who answered the phone, trying to keep my voice under control. "I was supposed to bring her home for the weekend, but I'm in bed with the flu—"

"Just a moment, Mrs. Brown. Mrs. Goldman is in today. She came in especially to talk to you since you were coming for Karen."

Mrs. Goldman was the supervisor. She didn't come to the school on Saturdays—unless something was wrong.

"Mrs. Brown, Karen is just fine, but there was an incident here last night."

"What was this incident, Mrs. Goldman?" All my nightmares were coming true. Numbly I heard her talking on and on, explaining, reassuring me.

"An intruder somehow got into the dormitory area where the girls sleep. He managed to take two girls to an empty floor . . . they escaped . . . told the night supervisor . . . meanwhile he went back to where Karen slept. . . ."

Out of a confused story, one thing came through clearly: my daughter had been taken away from her bed by an unknown man, and they had been found by the police in a stairwell between floors at eleven-thirty at night.

"Karen went to Bellevue last night for an examination, Mrs. Brown. We're certain that she wasn't actually molested. Please try to stay calm."

Small comfort to me. Actual or attempted, whatever, she had been subjected to a terrible experience. It was not easy to stay calm. I was close to hysteria.

"I'll be there to get her as soon as I can."

"I think both you and Mr. Brown ought to come here together and discuss what should be done," Mrs. Goldman said. "We're very upset about what's happened, and you'll have to decide whether you want to leave her here or not."

Of course I couldn't leave her there. I'd never have a night's sleep if she stayed.

"What happened to Karen is an unusual occurrence," Ann Coleman said when we met with her and Mrs. Goldman. "I don't think it will happen again. The school has tightened up security. If you decide to let her stay here, you can be sure nothing similar will ever occur."

Could I be sure? Maybe Ann could be, but I doubted that I could.

Mrs. Goldman added: "On the other hand, we know what a terrible experience this has been for you. I wouldn't blame you if you didn't want to leave her here. Incidents like this do occur from time to time in institutional settings."

I blazed out at them then, at their ambivalence. "How can

(186)

you say one thing and then exactly the opposite? What if it were your daughter? Do you mean to tell me that you'd consider for a moment leaving her where some pervert can walk in and molest crippled girls at will? This school is supported by taxpayers' money. You are paid by the tax-payers. How dare you allow anything like this to happen ever?"

I was in a frenzy of rage and hysteria, half-sobbing out all my violence and revulsion.

"None of you has to worry about Karen. I do—me. Every moment of my life. You can sit there and talk about this side of the question and that side and never once have to suffer the way I do. Yes, I'm going to take her home where she'll be safe, and if I can find a way to do it, I'm going to sue the state of New York, and you'll never have to think about Karen Brown again."

Now I was really hysterical.

"Please, Mrs. Brown, please stay calm. I know the school must bear some blame for this, if only because Karen was in its charge when it happened, but security was not espe-cially lax. It's an unfortunate fact of life in institutions and in the outside world that things like this do happen. What we're trying to decide now is whether Karen should continue to board here."

"I don't see that we have any choice," Richard said. "I don't see that we can leave her here."

Ann said: "If you take her home with you, she can still continue in our day program until it's time for camp. You're entitled to that. We have a bus that will pick her up in the morning and bring her home in the afternoon."

"And what am I supposed to do—work half-days for the next two months because I have to be a nursemaid to my twenty-year-old daughter?"

"If you can arrange for a nursemaid during the week, I think we can have the state pay for someone on the weekend," Ann said.

That meant I'd have to turn over my room to Karen and the nursemaid. I asked Richard if he would take her for the weekends so I could have some relief, and he agreed. At least I'll be able to sleep in my own bed two nights a week, I thought bitterly.

"All right," I said. "I'll get a housekeeper for weekdays at my apartment, and you take Karen on weekends."

"It's only for a few weeks," Ann said. "Everything is going to work out."

I had heard that a lot lately, and nothing had worked out yet.

Chapter 24

☙

Someone hit me on the knee," Karen told me when I brought her home. "I cried. I was sick and went to the hospital."

She was full of her story.

"Will I sleep with you for a long time?" she asked when I told her she was staying at home.

Too long, probably, I thought. "Yes," I said. I wondered how much the incident had upset her. I was still shaken by it myself, although after my outburst in Ann's office, I'd managed to calm myself down enough to notice that she seemed to be all right and that I was still feverish from the flu.

Wearily I tried to reach employment agencies and finally got a housekeeper-nursemaid to start on Monday.

"I like my school," Karen told me before the school bus picked her up on Monday. "I read at the school."

"Good," I said. "You read, and you come back here after lunch."

That seemed to please her. It didn't please me so much.

When the bus dropped her off in the afternoon, I was waiting on the curb to take her up to the nursemaid who had arrived with her suitcase and settled into my bedroom where she and Karen would sleep. I introduced them and rushed back to my office to finish the day. That night, while I tossed on the living room couch, I kept telling myself that I would survive the weeks ahead.

On Wednesday afternoon I had a call at the office from the nursemaid.

"Mrs. Brown, I've got to go back home. There's sickness in my family."

"When are you coming back?"

"I don't know. I don't think you can count on me. I've got to leave right away before the little girl gets home. You think you can come home to meet her?"

I couldn't, but I did.

The agency lined up another woman for the next day. On Thursday afternoon I was at home again, meeting another new woman with a suitcase. Karen got off the bus. I introduced them, threw them together in the apartment, and ran back to my job. Friday night, that woman left for the weekend, and a third one, sent by the state, appeared for the weekend. Karen's father hadn't called about taking her for the weekend as we'd agreed, but I was too weary to press it. I kept her with me.

The next day the weekday woman decided, for some

reason, that she had to leave, so I spent more time on the phone with the agency, who sent another woman who surveyed the problems of Karen calmly and stayed for a while.

The constant stream of live-in women made me a little edgy, as if I weren't in a turmoil already, just having Karen around. All of them had different eating habits and bathing habits, different sleeping habits and personalities. All liked to keep their clothes in different places in different ways. I who had lived alone for years suddenly had no privacy and a couch to sleep on. The latest nursemaid, much to my surprise, was apparently ready professionally to work at any moment of the day or night, since she slept in her wig. I remember once going into the bedroom to look at Karen, and seeing the woman asleep on the white couch, the white sheets pulled up to her chin, elaborate wig in place. She looked like someone laid out in a coffin.

By the end of the second week I was wondering if I would ever get through until it was time for Karen to go to camp. Whenever I was at home, Karen was at me constantly, pulling at me, hugging me, telling me about her day. The lack of discipline, her unstructured life, was beginning to tell on her and me.

I was counting the days until the weekend, when Karen would go to her father. Until she went to camp. Until I saw my doctor and I could pour out all my frustrations in the naive hope that overnight I would be made well and happy.

I was puzzled by the fact that I hadn't yet received a clothing list for camp or for school in the fall. It was already May. I finally called the school and spoke to a young man who turned out to be the camp director.

"Just a minute," he said. "I'm looking at the camp list, and I don't see a Karen Brown on it."

"It was all arranged weeks ago."

"I'm afraid I don't know anything about your child. The head of the school isn't here today. I'll have her call you tomorrow."

Right away, I knew something was wrong.

I called Ann Coleman. "What does it mean?"

"I'll call her," Ann said. "I'll let you know what she says on Monday."

Karen, at home and full of her day at school, was less appealing to me than she had ever been. The nursemaid was packing up for her weekend off. The weekend lady was at the door. Karen's arms were twined around my neck and she was chattering away in her silent language that seemed as loud and grating as a roomful of shrieking children.

"Karen, leave me alone. Mother's tired."

"My school . . . my daddy . . . my brother . . ." New words, questions, teachers. She wouldn't stop.

"You will see your daddy tomorrow. Now go watch television."

Karen's father hadn't called by Saturday morning. When I called his apartment, there was no answer. The woman from the camp hadn't called me back.

"Please," I said to the weekend woman, "take her into the bedroom and watch television with her. I want to lie down for a while."

Saturday passed. Sunday. With increasing frequency, as soon as I lay down on my makeshift bed in the living room, Karen would creep from the bedroom and crawl onto the couch with me.

"Go back to the bedroom."

"I want to sleep with you."

"Stop crying and go to your room."

"I want to sleep with you. I want to see my daddy."

I wasn't a woman who had just given birth to a baby, yet

I had a baby to care for. She hadn't lived at home for twelve years and now I was spending all my hours at home attending to her. As soon as I walked into the house, she would throw herself at me. If I went into a room and closed the door, she lay on the floor and tried to peek under the door or pounded on it until I let her in. If I sat down in the kitchen to eat, she was in my lap. She couldn't be blamed for what she did, but it became harder and harder for me to take.

On Monday Ann called, and it wasn't all right.

"The school isn't going to take Karen after all. The director said the staff decided she wouldn't fit in. She'd be too much for them."

"But we were promised—"

"I'm sorry."

"What am I going to do? I'll go crazy if I have to have her around much longer." The tears wouldn't stop.

"I'll start making more calls right away. There's a camp for the handicapped that I know will take her."

"And after that?"

"We'll keep at it."

This time she didn't say, "Don't worry." There was no point in it. I was dreadfully worried. I tottered through the week between two equally miserable visions of the future: on one hand, Karen in a huge state institution like the one that haunted my dreams, the only place willing to take her; and on the other, Karen living at home with me, as we had been living the past couple of weeks, growing old and older together, with me hating her more each day, until I died, and Karen was left to—what? A state institution?

The doctor said soothing things, telling me it wasn't as bad as it seemed.

"It's worse," I said. "You haven't been through what I have. Nothing happens easily in the kind of world Karen and I live in. You don't have to live with her. Every moment

(193)

I'm home is pure agony. Last night, I paid thirty-six dollars to stay at a hotel so I could get a night's sleep."

On Thursday morning the nursemaid asked if she could be away that night; she'd be back early in the morning.

"All right. I can manage." I was on the ragged edge of despair. I didn't really care. Besides, I was planning to call Richard and beg him, if necessary, to take her and the weekend woman for the weekend, as he had promised. I was anticipating those forty-eight hours of peace. Also, seeing her father would calm Karen down.

"When are you coming to get Karen for the weekend?" I asked him when I finally reached him on Thursday night. "I thought you were taking her last weekend, but I couldn't get you."

"I'm not coming. I can't."

"What do you mean, you *can't*?"

"I mean, I can't bring her to this apartment. My wife isn't up to having her here overnight. If you like, I'll take her for the afternoon on Saturday, for lunch, but she can't stay here for the weekend."

"You can't do that to me. You promised."

"I promised before I'd talked to my wife. It won't be convenient to have Karen here."

"But you promised—" I couldn't seem to talk to anyone any more without crying.

"I'm not going to argue with my wife," he said. "I've been arguing with her all week about this."

I went out of control, screaming, crying, because I was only holding myself together until the weekend. I damned Karen's father to hell, and slammed down the receiver.

I was living in a household where every night about twelve or one o'clock, Karen would wake herself up and stand beside the couch where I was sleeping, and sob and beg to sleep with me, to see her father. She'd force my eyes open so that I could see her hand signs, and sob some more. She was, I see now, really disturbed for the first time in her life and was taking it out on me. She felt displaced. She didn't know what was happening to her: changing schools and being molested at one of them; constantly changing nursemaids; the lack of discipline; a mother who was unfit to deal with her calmly and a father who wouldn't see her. She was clutching at me for dear life, holding on, and I had no one to hold onto.

"Go to the bedroom, Karen, and watch television."

"I want to stay here."

"No. You be quiet in the bedroom. Mother wants to sleep."

She puckered up her face to cry.

"No crying. You only smile. Forget about crying."

I lay back on the couch closed my eyes. Karen was beside me, forcing my eyelids open.

"My daddy," she started. "When will I see my daddy?"

How was I going to tell her that she wasn't going to see him?

"You'll see him later. Go away."

"How many days?"

"Go away. Forget about your daddy. Leave me alone."

She dragged herself away to the bedroom. She was back in half an hour, pulling, crying, knocking things off tables, stumbling around the room, pushing my eyes open. The tears streamed down her cheeks. She was doing everything she could to make me acknowledge her.

It was a test of wills now, totally irrational, each of us determined to have her own way. I finally took her by the hand and dragged her back into the bedroom.

"Sit there," I screamed. "Be quiet. Leave me alone."

Karen looked at me with a combination of fear and stubbornness.

(195)

I was sobbing when I returned to the living room.

"No!" I screamed the second her fingers touched my eyelids. "No, no, no!"

I grabbed a handful of her hair, twisting it, still screaming, "Leave me alone."

Karen was on her knees, sobbing, uttering horrible, incoherent sounds, but fighting back as well as she could, clutching my legs as hard as her crippled hands could manage.

I started to drag her across the living room to the bedroom by her hair. "Leave me alone, or I'll kill you. I'll kill both of us." I started to slap her. If she was knocked senseless, she would be quiet.

Karen struggled and fought back, but I was in the grip of an uncontrolled frenzy. I would beat her and beat her with all the fury and rage and grief and suffering that had been in me for twenty years.

The living room window, only three steps away, looked down twenty-five stories to the street. All I would have to do would be to lean out of that window until I fell.

"I'm going crazy. I have to stop." But I didn't stop. I didn't let go of that struggling, crippled, deaf, retarded child who had marked my life so cruelly, whom I had struggled to keep alive and well. I wasn't going to let go of her until she was dead and my sufferings were ended.

Then Karen slumped to the floor and looked up at me with terror. Her hysterical crying turned into deep, deep sobs. She was afraid. Afraid of her own mother.

Somehow my sanity returned and I grabbed the phone. My hands were trembling so badly that I could hardly dial.

"Come quickly, Claudette," I sobbed. "I almost killed Karen. I don't even know if she's all right. Help me, help me, please."

"I'll be right there," she said. "Sit down and don't move.

Call your doctor. Will you do that? Will you call him and wait for me?"

"Yes." I could barely speak. "Hurry."

"It's an emergency," I told the doctor's answering service. "It's life and death. Please, please try to reach him."

Claudette arrived to find me huddled in the dark living room, in the midst of the wreckage I had caused. Karen was sitting on the bedroom floor, weeping uncontrollably.

The phone rang. Claudette spoke to the doctor. He was on his way. She got Karen to lie down in the bedroom while she sat with me in the living room. The doctor arrived. I was exhausted. He gave me something that made me drowsy. I let Claudette persuade me to lie down. The doctor looked in on Karen. Claudette promised to stay the night. Ann Coleman arrived. I didn't remember calling her. The three of them talked together in a corner. The doctor and Ann left.

Karen slept from exhaustion. With the help of the sedative, I slept through the worst night of my life.

Chapter 25

꩜

CLAUDETTE WAS WITH ME when I woke the next morning. I felt drained and depressed, but no longer murderous or suicidal. The nursemaid came in, looked at the damage in the living room, and talked to Claudette for a moment.

"She's getting Karen ready for school," Claudette said. "Are you feeling better?"

"Yes. Is Karen?"

"She's quiet. I gave her breakfast in the bedroom."

I started to cry. "You're so good to us. I might have killed her."

"You didn't, and you wouldn't have. Are you going to work today?"

"Yes, I have to. . . . Claudette, I can't ever lose control like that again. I don't ever want to come that close. That window is twenty-five stories up. I was ready to jump."

"You're sure you'll be all right?"

"I'm OK now. You go to your job. I can't keep you here all day."

"Your doctor wants you to call as soon as you can. And Mrs. Coleman. Call me if you need me."

I knew now that not only did I have to figure out what to do about Karen, I had to figure out what to do about myself. I had been thinking that it was only Karen and the circumstances of her life that had caused all the trouble in my life. Now I saw that a lot of my trouble had been caused by me. When I looked in the mirror that morning, I admitted to myself that I needed help to put my life back together. I hoped there might still be time to do so.

For the first time, alone in the shambles of my apartment and my life, I understood that this was what the doctor had been trying to make me see. He knew that he wasn't just a prop to hold me up until I found a school for Karen. He was trying to help me rebuild myself so that there would be no need for props.

"There has to be a place in this world for both Karen and me," I thought as I put on my prettiest dress and spent a long time on my makeup and hair. I was going to make the outside of me as attractive as possible, because I alone knew what the inside was like.

"Are you all right?" Ann Coleman asked when I called her later that day.

"I'm alive, she's alive."

"I've gotten Karen into a camp," she told me. "You don't have to do anything but fill out some forms. There's no chance she'll be rejected at the last minute. They take people much worse off than she is."

All I could think of was the day she would finally be gone, when the nursemaids would go away. I still didn't know what I would do with her when the eight weeks of camp were over, but I knew she would never live at home again.

In the remaining weeks she was with me after that terrible night, I kept away from her as much as possible. Often I spent only an hour with her in the evening, and went away to spend the night elsewhere, abandoning my home and child to the nursemaid who dealt serenely with her and kept the house in order. In this way we got through the spring. Finally the day came when I took her to Fourteenth Street to get the camp bus. I watched her that day, stumbling around, making friends, behaving as much like a normal person as she could. I saw those children from the long-ago days at the Cerebral Palsy Center and their prematurely aged parents, none of them with Karen's interest in life. Through the numbness created by living with Karen during those long weeks, I saw that I had made possible the vital young woman in front of me. I could be proud of that. I had done my job with Karen. Now I needed only to find a safe, permanent haven for her. Only then could I start to find a haven for myself.

That kind of haven meant a man I loved, who loved me. If only I could start out fresh, the way I did with Richard and have my happy ending twenty years later.

"Why have you never remarried?" my doctor asked me.

"A lot of people have asked me that. I should think it would be obvious. I've never met a man I could marry. None of them wanted to marry me."

"Why do you feel that way? You're an attractive woman. You have a pleasing personality. Why do you suppose no one wants to marry you?"

"They had all kinds of reasons. Paul was young, too young, I see now. He couldn't deal with Karen. Alan was a mess. The others, well, I never got very serious about them."

"Yet you want to marry again."

"Maybe I just don't deserve that kind of happiness. Maybe I was meant to be alone."

"Nonsense. There's no law written down any place that says certain people are meant to be happily married, while others are meant to be lonely. Who do you suppose *meant* you to be alone? Not to remarry?"

"Those men I cared about made it impossible."

"How so? By not being exactly what you thought they should be?"

"Are you trying to tell me that *I* made it impossible? I handled things very well. It was just that I had so many responsibilities, with Karen always there in the background."

"Karen was your excuse. This Alan got on well with Karen, yet he was obviously a sick man. Yet you maintained the relationship."

"I guess I deserved the kind of punishment I took from Alan—"

"Deserved?"

"I'm not a very good person. I'm terrible, in fact. Didn't I try to kill her one night? I gave birth to that child and after I loved her and made her live, I sent her away, abandoned her. I hurt my husband because I couldn't force him to become the man of my beautiful dream. In some way, I'm guilty of my mother's death, even my father's. I feel guilty about my son and the kind of life I've given him. Sometimes I feel guilty about being alive. If I can have enough misery in my life, and have men who mistreat me, destructive relationships like Alan's, then I'm getting what I deserve."

The doctor looked at me, and then I looked at myself.

"You're right, of course," I said slowly. "They have all been impossible men, losers, people I could look at with contempt when they didn't want to marry me, because they weren't worth it, and I wasn't worth anything. It was a way of protecting myself from being hurt even worse. What if he turned out to be perfect for me, and he still didn't marry me? I don't know what I'd do."

"I don't know either. Why don't you risk looking for him and find out?"

That summer, as the doctor slowly helped me untie the knots of confusion and guilt inside me, was not a time to think about my personal life. I was writing letters to every school I could locate, in New York and out of state. September was getting closer.

"Please consider her," I begged. "Karen can do a lot of things, even though she is deaf and physically and mentally handicapped." I enclosed reports by her speech and hearing therapists, evaluations of her abilities, and recommendations that she be given the opportunity to continue in a learning situation.

I got back every kind of reply imaginable:

"Yes, we will accept her." For an astronomical amount of money. It takes a high income indeed to be able to afford ten thousand dollars a year for her care for the next forty or fifty years of her life.

"We take no deaf children."

"We only accept children who are one hundred percent self-sufficient and ambulatory."

"We have a minimum IQ for children we accept."

No this, no that. Hope dimmed with every answer I received. I knew that whatever progress I was making with my doctor would be canceled out the day I had to send Karen to a state institution.

I sent letters to Florida, to California, to Iowa, to Pennsylvania, Connecticut, and New Jersey. I spent the whole summer talking to Ann Coleman, to schools around the country, to my doctor, to anyone who could possibly help me. I went through my old file of letters, written over the years to different schools, and wrote them again. There was one in Pennsylvania, an all-girl school that kept children into their adult years. It had a good program. At the time, Karen hadn't been accepted because of a long waiting list. There was another in New Jersey for which Karen had been too young at the time. There was a third in Florida that said they had a building program underway, and couldn't say when there would be an opening for her.

I sent out the last group of letters, then left for California on business for two weeks. I had done everything in my power for Karen. Ann Coleman had done everything she could. I had made every telephone call, written every letter anyone had suggested. Now I prayed.

I prayed the way I had years before when Karen was a tiny girl and I knew that I had to give her up. I prayed then for the strength to do it. Now I prayed again, remembering that out of nowhere those long years ago, strength and help had come to me.

My trip took me to Hollywood, Beverly Hills, to my moments of stardom among stars, to people who knew nothing about my private sorrow, to whom I was a visitor from glamorous New York.

When I returned, my mailbox was stuffed with replies.

A pile of no's, but in a blue envelope postmarked Florida, the magic letter I had been praying for:

"We are glad to hear from you. We certainly do remember your earlier letter about Karen. Our situation has changed since you last wrote us. We have a place for Karen. We are sure we can make Karen happy and comfortable, and we look forward to seeing both of you."

I went to bed that night, holding onto that letter. I carried it with me for ten days, taking it out from time to time to read it for some hidden meaning between the lines. I didn't tell anyone about it—not Ann Coleman, nor my doctor, nor Claudette.

I read and reread the brochure, which said that the school took children regardless of race, creed, IQ, or physical disability; they would take anyone. That meant they certainly would take Karen. I tried to see from the pictures if the place looked all right: a group of children, some palm trees, a couple of buildings. Still I didn't call the school or write. I knew I was deliberately ruining my one chance in the world for Karen because I was simply paralyzed.

A second letter arrived from Florida: "Since you haven't replied to our first letter, perhaps you are no longer interested in sending Karen to us. . . ."

I was on the phone at once: "I've been out of town," I lied. "I'm coming to see you next week. Please keep the place for Karen. She'll be home from camp in a couple of weeks."

"This is your school," I told a tanned and healthy Karen, showing her the brochure from Florida. I'd been there for a day to look at it, and it seemed perfect: clean and shining, the sun was out, there were palm trees and blue sky, happy children, with all kinds of handicaps. Karen would never be a problem to them.

"We're going to fly there on a plane."

That didn't make her very happy. She had been on a plane once and didn't like it.

"You'll sleep there. They will love you."

How many times had I told her that lately? She never seemed to sleep very long at any of these schools that were supposed to love her so much.

"I want to stay with you." But it was halfhearted. Somehow she never got to sleep very long with me either.

"Will you call me? Will you write to me? Will you visit me? How many days until I see you?"

"Forget about days. We are going to pack your suitcase."

More new dresses and shorts and shoes. A new bathing suit. Karen didn't like the looks of that. She'd had a bad time with a swimming pool once. Swimming wasn't her idea of fun.

That night, before we went to bed, Karen went to the packed suitcase and rummaged around until she found the bathing suit.

"Forget about swimming," she said, holding up the suit. "I'm not ever swimming again."

She stood on tiptoes and stuffed the bathing suit away on the top shelf of the armoire. It was hidden now, far away; there was no way it would get back in her suitcase. While she slept, I put the bathing suit back into the suitcase, under all her clothes. Once she was in Florida, she would be interested in swimming.

The next morning I was washing my hair in the tub when Karen burst into the bathroom, clutching the bathing suit.

She was outraged. "I told you to forget about swimming!" she said.

I laughed and laughed while the shampoo on my head

dripped into my eyes. Karen, though not quite sure of the joke, laughed with me.

Then Karen—my daughter, twenty-one, hopeless to all except me—knelt beside the tub and gently began to wash my hair.

Epilogue

❦

EVERYBODY wants happy endings. I have a few that give me satisfaction. My dream of becoming the editor of a national magazine came true. This year I also saw my son graduate from college, a handsome, humorous, capable young man of whom I am very proud. His life hasn't been easy, yet he has survived the difficulties that have confronted him since he was born. He is, perhaps, my happiest ending.

After several years of therapy I felt myself able to stand alone without the support of my doctor. I had first grasped at the help therapy offered, to get me through the nightmare of finding a school for Karen and dealing with the terrible events of that period. In the process I discovered and came to terms with myself. This new knowledge helped me to find a kind of peace that I could not have discovered alone. To be free of the anxiety that has been a part of my life for years is almost a happy enough ending in itself.

I can visit my daughter in Florida and see her well and healthy, surrounded by a devoted staff and other happy children. I welcome the Mother's Day and birthday cards on which she has laboriously printed her name, and the notes from the school that tell me she joins in the activities and sits quietly during the story hour "as if she could hear every word."

I have been able, moreover, to separate myself from her emotionally and physically, so both of us can live. I have learned to accept that Karen doesn't have a lot of living left to do, while I still have a great deal.

Karen will never "improve," and she may even deteriorate. There is no guarantee that her condition will remain stable for the next forty or so years of her life. Any day another fateful telephone call may come, and she will be pushed again into the center of my life. I hope that I am better prepared than I once was to face it.

My problems are never solved, nor are those of other parents of handicapped children. What of those who have not had the opportunities (and in some cases, good luck) that I have had? What kinds of decisions must these other parents make? What advice must they weigh? What kind of help is there for them? The truth is: very little. I know from experience that there are few institutions capable of dealing with children like Karen, those with multiple handicaps. Public institutions remain, in general, unsatisfactory, while the private ones are, all too often, far beyond the means of most people. The agencies that are supposed to aid the handicapped are seldom adequate for the urgent needs of the individual and his or her family. The existence of such a child tests the spirit and strength of a family; few can bear the strain.

And there remains the problem that haunts my every day and night: who will care for Karen when I am gone? The state? The federal government? The uncertainty plays a part in all my efforts to make her present life as happy as possible.

My story of Karen has, at this moment, a happy ending; but there are no genuinely happy endings for the physically and mentally impaired and their families. We can only try to carry the burden that has been given to us, that changes us, and that makes our lives different.